GOVERNANCE:
A CHALLENGE TO SMALL CHURCHES
A Practical Guide to Church Administration

Rev. Dr. Rakar Williams, JP

Governance: A Challenge to Small Churches.
Copyright © 2018. Rev. Dr. Rakar Williams, JP.
All Rights Reserved.

Printed in the United States of America.

No portion of this book may be reproduced, stored in a retrieval system, or transmitted in any form or by any means, except for brief quotations in printed reviews, without the prior written permission of Rev. Dr. Rakar Williams and DayeLight Publishers.

Unless otherwise indicated, all scripture quotations are taken from the King James Version.

Book Cover Design by HCP Book Publishing

ISBN: 978-1-949343-22-9

DEDICATION

TO MY FAMILY

God has blessed me with a very supportive wife and three lovely, talented children. I am privileged to have their love and affection, and overall, they make my life complete. While completing my dissertation for a doctorate in business administration, they were of much help and encouragement. The dissertation was dedicated to them, and similarly, I dedicate this book to them as it contains many extracts and excerpts from the dissertation. So, with gratitude, I devote this book to my wife, Joy Roberts-Williams, and my children: Rochelle, Rakar Jr., and Rajay. They have been patient, understanding, and very excited at my achievement.

May God bless my family continually and keep us in His presence at all times.

Acknowledgments

I wholeheartedly recognize all the people who contributed to the development and completion of my dissertation. Their role was important to that exercise, from which I can now benefit in producing this book. Gratitude is hereby expressed to the faculty members of Swiss Management Center University, especially Dr. Peter Kiriakidis; Prof. Saifuddin Rangwala; Ms. Marilyn Baker, Administrator; and Professor Adrian Ravier, Dissertation Supervisor. Also, I am forever grateful to Mrs. Alison Peart, Retired Senior Vice Principal of Excelsior High School.

I express heartfelt thanks to all the churches and pastors who participated in the study, and special thanks to my family and those who worked with me in completing this book. For every encouragement, every critical thought or comment, or for just being there, I thank you.

In particular, I specially recognise the leaders and members of the Model Church of God, where I serve as the Overseer, for their heartfelt support.

My journey in leadership, both professionally and in ministry, has been interesting and sometimes challenging, but *"the hand of God has never led me to any place that His grace was not able to keep me,"* so for that, I am grateful to God. I thank God for His enabling power and for His Spirit that continues to guide me day by day.

Foreword

The application of scientific approaches to management is truly imperative to the success of the local church. This application is an insightful paradigm shift in the context of the ecclesiastical community and demonstrates how the Holy Spirit is working in a contemporary and modernistic way.

Most churches consider lack of growth and under-engagement in missions to be a factor of insufficient spirituality. More specifically, this factor involves inadequate periods of prayer and Scripture-reading, and not being filled with the Spirit. Here, Dr. Williams provides alternative ideas about the hindrances to success in the church and addresses these and other hindrances scholastically and innovatively.

Small churches that apply what I will call the "Williams Church Management Principles" will identify problem areas and strengthen the membership, which are Dr. Williams' stated objectives. Moreover, churches that apply these principles will improve their governance structures and procedures and will better detect gaps in membership development. Dr. Williams also provides solutions to identified issues by recommending leadership principles, practices, and procedures that have proven effective [as evidenced in his research] and that will facilitate the growth and better administration of the small church.

The value of the concepts presented in this book for the local church and the imperative of implementing its contents cannot be overstated. Reader response will add the spontaneous unwritten chapter of this book. This response is summed up in the quote at the start of Chapter 12, and I encourage you to begin actualizing that unwritten chapter today.

Bishop Dr. Alvin R. Bailey
Senior Pastor of the Portmore
Holiness Christian Church

Presiding Bishop of
the Holiness Christian Church Inc.

ABSTRACT

Corporate governance is an important phenomenon in the business sector, but to a lesser extent within churches. The Bible speaks of administration but not corporate governance; however, these are used interchangeably in business sectors and likewise in this book. A study was conducted primarily to gain an understanding of corporate governance within the small churches in Jamaica. The views of ten pastors were sought, describing their experience of corporate governance in the church. This was a purposeful sampling to assess the viewpoints of the leaders from a variety of denominations.

The researcher used structured interviews and reviewed the churches' archival data. Based on the results, 40% of the churches are operating illegally, as they were not adhering to the regulatory requirements of Jamaica. Responses indicate mixed themes relating to accountability;

the majority of the participants believe corporate governance can eliminate destructive conflicts, and the respondents are of the view that it is possible for churches to implement better governance practices. Additionally, there is poor succession planning in place, unacceptable storing of the church documents, and issues regarding the ownership of land. Further research is needed to explore the reasons for non-compliance of some churches and the likely impact on the membership when the governance structure is not being reviewed periodically. Where the church pays greater attention to corporate governance, the likely result is growth, better controls, and successful outcomes.

TABLE OF CONTENTS

Foreword vii
Abstract ix
Chapter 1   Introduction 1
Chapter 2   Corporate Governance 11
Chapter 3   Registration of Church 21
Chapter 4   Statutory Obligation 31
Chapter 5   Codes of Best Practices.................41
Chapter 6   Administration 47
Chapter 7   Leadership and
            Strategic Planning.........................55
Chapter 8   Succession Planning......................63
Chapter 9   Accountability 71
Chapter 10 Recordkeeping.............................77
Chapter 11 Acquisition of Assets 85
Chapter 12 Establishing a Board.....................93

Chapter 13	Importance of Meeting 101
Chapter 14	Risk Management 111
Chapter 15	Dealing with Destructive Conflicts 125
Chapter 16	Network among Churches 139
References	 143

Chapter 1
Introduction

"Twenty years from now you will be more disappointed by the things that you didn't do than by the ones you did do. So throw off the bowlines. Sail away from the safe harbour. Catch the trade winds in your sails. Explore. Dream. Discover."

~ Mark Twain

This book seeks to reveal extracts and insights gained from a dissertation completed for a doctorate in business administration. The abstract gives a summary of the study; however, not all areas of the study will be revealed in this book. Suffice it to say, this book is a must read and a keepsake for pastors, administrators, and treasurers of the church. It can also be helpful to small business operators, as the content covers some critical issues of governance. Although the content of this book focuses primarily on Jamaica, the information can be used by people of other jurisdictions as a foundation. The information can point business operators to some critical issues to be mindful of, wherever they operate on the globe.

Nieuwhof (2015) highlighted five signs that bad governance is stifling your church's growth and mission, but many churches are not paying attention to these signs. These signs are as follows:

1. *Your board or congregation loves to micromanage.*
2. *Your congregation demands consensus.*
3. *Your board or congregation doesn't trust the staff.*
4. *Your staff hates the board.*
5. *Your board focuses on complainers.*

In Jamaica, there is a large population of churches (Scott-Williams, 2011). There is no real evidence that these churches have effective governance practices, especially the small churches. Similarly, there are various denominations and beliefs among the churches (Chisholm, 2012). Based on Drucker (1990), nonprofit organizations in

America have almost limitless diversity in their mission and size, but the majority have the same governance structure. A question, then, is whether all small churches in Jamaica could have the same governance structure.

According to the STATIN 2011 Population and Housing Census, Jamaica's population is 2.7 million, and Christianity is the predominant religion (Chisholm, 2012). Nevertheless, there is variation among the churches in terms of doctrine and beliefs. A high possibility exists that these figures and comments from Chisholm have not properly documented and communicated sufficient information about small churches.

Churches in Jamaica have the autonomy and freedom to a great extent because the government does not impose strict regulations. It is possible this freedom could be abused, especially if basic guidelines are not provided. There are many unreported instances of poor administration of church funds in Jamaica. Bakker (2011) highlighted examples on how attention is needed regarding poor administration.

Many small Jamaican churches started as family churches or with one person leading, thus raising concerns as to its sustainability and accountability. Prior studies in this area have proven limited. However, Oakley and Russett (2004) looked at governance in the past and stated that the early church was a community in which all participated in community life. They also discussed a mixed constitution for the church. In concluding, they posited that the modern practices of representation and consent that characterize secular constitutional government are not aligned with the tradition of the church.

Many small churches tend to be in breach of Jamaica's regulatory requirements, as churches are expected to be registered with the Companies Office of Jamaica. In 2009, the government of Jamaica had to launch an amnesty to regularize the churches. Notwithstanding, some churches are still not registered. This could be because of the views being held by church leaders concerning the relevance of the regulatory requirements, or simply ignorance. There is a general view that small churches in Jamaica place greater emphasis on spiritual aspects while neglecting or paying little attention to the business aspects. Still, not enough is known about the impact of non-registration on the small churches' operations and its link to improve corporate governance.

When a business, including the church, is not registered as a legal entity, it operates contrary to the 2004 Companies Act, which is used by The Companies Office of Jamaica to regulate the operations of businesses in Jamaica. The possibility exists that inappropriate actions, such as money laundering, can be present in churches where accountability is not being enforced. The non-registration of the church implies that the church will not be in a position to acquire assets in its name, so, technically, the trustee(s) whose names were used to purchase the asset(s) may be deemed the legal owner(s).

The relevance of statutory and legislative requirements concerning the church will be presented, with a view to bringing about a greater awareness to church leaders. Most importantly, the views of 10 small church leaders are presented throughout the book, which is to serve as a reference to other church leaders of similar churches, especially those struggling with the administrative arm of their respective churches.

The focus of this book is on the small church. Therefore, it is important to have a foundation on what constitutes a small church. According to USA Church (2014), a small church is one that has an average weekend attendance of fewer than 50 people. According to Dudley (2003), small churches struggle for membership, money, and survival. Dudley shared different perspectives of defining small churches. First, money becomes a frequent criterion in defining the small church, and so a small church may be defined as those congregations with 250 or fewer communicant members. Second, churches averaging fewer than 45 members in attendance should be classified as small. For the purpose of this book, a small church is considered a Christian denomination operating as an individual church in one location with a membership of less than 200 people, or a Christian denomination with up to ten branches with the collective membership being no more than 300 people.

Small membership churches differ from large churches in ways other than size (Killen, 2005). There are different kinds of organisms that live and grow differently. Furthermore, committed and creative pastors seek appropriate and effective ways of doing ministry in their own church and community.

In the dissertation, the researcher set out to examine corporate governance within ten small churches in Jamaica by focusing on the following research questions:

Question 1: *What do the church leaders perceive are some of the problems caused by poor governance procedures within small churches?*

The anticipation of the study outcomes was that greater attention will be given to governance within these churches. Therefore, the interviews zeroed in on the possibility of problems caused by poor governance, looking at them from the lenses of the pastors, once there is evidence of poor governance procedures.

Question 2*: To what extent are church leaders aware of how these problems impact the membership of the church in terms of growth?*

Inherent problems are possibly affecting the membership growth of the church, but pastors may not be mindful of this. This question called upon each pastor to take a critical look at his/her church and to share his/her views on this crucial matter. For the sustainability of these churches, it is expected that each pastor would pay keen attention to issues that could affect the membership growth.

Question 3: *What do church leaders perceive it would take to strengthen the governance procedures of their respective church?*

The knowledge of how to strengthen the governance structure of an organization is very important. This question aimed to get the views of the pastors on how they as leaders would approach curbing problems identified because of a poor governance structure. The anticipated outcome was that the information shared could be useful not just to that church but to any church facing a similar situation.

It is hoped that the details shared will benefit the wider church body, as it will cover corporate governance, succession planning, decision-making, administration, leadership, and the Companies Act (2004), among other areas. The work of various authors supported the discussion and, hence, are included in this book. These are some critical areas to be considered regarding corporate governance within small churches. By assessing these, a small church could be impacted as follows:

1) The church could restructure its corporate governance to improve effectiveness.
2) The leader(s) of the church could gain insights on the various factors necessary for sound governance practice.

3) The leader of the church's views on corporate governance could be enhanced, especially on how it can affect the growth of the church.
4) The role and relevance of stakeholders in the church will be highlighted.
5) The benefits to be derived if the churches could adhere to proper corporate governance would be emphasized.

During the defense stage of the dissertation, one panelist questioned the relevance of risk management to the church as a part of the corporate governance model. It was then that I realized I left out a very critical aspect on my assessment. As such, this will be dealt with exclusively, but not in relation to the study done for the dissertation.

SUMMARY OF GUIDELINES

1) Good administration/governance includes being registered – adhering to a regulatory framework and guidelines.

2) An effective Board should be in place that will steer the church and eliminate the one-man approach.

3) Keen attention to the administration of finances is needed at all times.

4) In addition to the spiritual arm, attention must be given to legal issues and possible risks.

5) It is crucial to have documented procedures and rules of operation. This should be clearly presented and known by all stakeholders.

Corporate Governance

*"If you can find a path with no obstacle,
it probably doesn't lead anywhere."*

~ Frank Clark

Corporate governance is a major facet of the business arena, and it is proving just as relevant to churches.[1] There have been several scandals pertaining to the misappropriation of funds and other issues that speak to the need for leaders of churches to implement a best practice governance structure (Elson et al., 2007).

Given the history of the misappropriation of funds and other issues highlighted by Elson et al., I

---

1 Elson, O'Callaghan, & Walker, 2007; McMurray, Islam, Sarros, & Pirola-Merlo, 2012

concur that corporate governance is imperative for the church and not just business as a whole. Good governance helps minimize problems that could cause embarrassment for the church and its members. Good governance demonstrates that leaders take their role seriously, and this could help in protecting the organization from possible attacks that could destroy the organization significantly.

Non-listed companies that operate under a well-designed and effective governance structure are likely to perform better and, consequently, will be more attractive to external investors (McCahery & Vermeulen, 2010). Harrington and Bertin (2009) indicated that the lack of sound corporate governance in the public and private sectors has enabled bribery, capitalism, and corruption to flourish throughout the world, suppressing sound and sustainable economic decisions.

Harrington and Bertin, in dealing with corporate governance for small to medium-sized organizations, define it as the relationship between a company's management, its Board, shareholders, and other stakeholders. They further stated that it provides the structure through which the objectives of the company are set, the means of attaining those objectives, and how to monitor performance.

In nonprofit organizations, corporate governance focuses on the organizational level of governance and on boards and their behavior (Cornforth, 2012). This also refers to arrangements of guidance and supervision (Siebart & Reichard, 2004). The basic requirements of corporate governance in a nonprofit organization include ensuring the organization has a clear mission and strategy and that the organization is well managed (Anheier, 2005).

Corporate governance is attracting considerable attention from many stakeholders.[2] This includes policy-makers, lawmakers, company executives, shareholders, banks and other investors, the media, legal and financial professionals, politicians, and regulatory bodies. Incidentally, Gregg (2001) considered "stakeholderism" an ethical theory of corporate governance, and, therefore, it is an incoherent and implausible guide to how corporations should act. Corporate governance is one specific and important focus of contemporary business ethics (Capaldi, 2005). Thus, its purpose is to persuade, induce, compel, and otherwise motivate corporate managers to keep the promises they make to investors (Macey, 2011).

---

2 Hambrick, Werder, & Zajac, 2008; McCahery & Vermeulen, 2010

The term corporate governance is internationally accepted, but the actual systems of corporate governance operating in different countries vary substantially (Channon, 1999). The reason for the variation is based on the various historical corporate development systems of the countries. We can presume this is so because of the differences among countries, which includes political, social, cultural, and other differences.

Channon also stated that interest in corporate governance has heightened because of the realization that it has a bearing on competitive position. Over time, the development of common systems is expected because of the growing development of global industries and the emergence of economic blocks.

Oakley and Russett (2004) looked at governance and accountability in the Catholic Church, noting that it is pertinent for the church today. Swartley (2005) ascribed to a thorough Biblical form of church governance, thus uncritical assimilation of secular management principles is rejected. Yet, he believes much can be learned from studies of management methods and that it is unwise to ignore empirical research.

In assessing the view of Swartley (2005) regarding the rejection of "secular management principles," we should remember that we operate in a political and cultural arena, so we must be mindful of this. People management skills are critical to any organization, and some of these "secular management principles" are what business operators, some of who are Christians, use to effectively run their business. It is imperative that we do not operate with a tunnel view but that we are cognizant of the broader picture and issues that impact the business. Furthermore, the church could set the standard for its individual members, who have to exist in this same political and cultural context in which the church operates.

Simpson (2008) contended that there has been a resurgence of interest in questions of accountability and governance among non-governmental organizations. It is clear that non-governmental organizations are treating the broad area of corporate governance as an important tool in their business success.

Channon (1999) highlighted that the system of governance moves along a continuum: individual–collegiate; confrontational–cooperation; selfish–sense of social obligation; legalistic–bound by honor and obligation; short-term, impatient–long-term, patient; and rigid, hierarchical–flexible. This clearly indicates that there are different systems of governance structure. Furthermore, some of these descriptions are not expected in the church, such as selfishness, confrontation, and impatience, so church leaders must be mindful of this when crafting a suitable corporate governance structure. Thomlinson (2006) stated that it doesn't really matter what kind of governance structure exists if only a few people take the trouble to understand and engage it.

Another key principle of corporate governance is that the executive management should be accountable for its actions (Channon, 1999). The management of executive accountability tends to fall on the non-executive directors. A Board comprising a mix of in-house leaders and other external leaders will generate greater governance (Gillan, 2006). Similarly, Kerr (2005) posited that Board independence can be positively influenced by having a majority of outside (non-executive) directors who are independent. Long (2008) stated that it is a best practice for private employee stock ownership plan (ESOP) companies, just like public companies, to seek outside directors to fulfill the board's role of oversight and strategic direction for the company.

Good corporate governance is achieved when the Board of Directors is controlling, directing, and/or monitoring to ensure long-term survival; play their roles effectively, honor corporate obligations and demonstrate responsible corporate social citizenship in all its business affairs and the community at large (Kerr, 2005). Harrington and Bertin (2009) reiterate the need for organizations to have a Board of Directors, to serve as a watchdog. Harrington and Bertin (2009) noted that the survival and growth of any organization depends on its owners and the Board's ability to evolve and adapt to changing business environments. Consequently, the church must be prepared for such changes, as failure to do so could result in the business arm of the church not being managed in the way it should.

Good corporate governance characteristics include transparency, accountability, probability, and protection of minority shareholders (Harrington & Bertin, 2009). Thus, governance is based on three cornerstone principles: ownership, stewardship, and accountability. In addition to the focus on corporate governance, the church's code of best practices, which should be evident in a good governance structure, must also be considered.

As we progress through this book, these critical issues will be discussed. Some of the issues may seem foreign to the church; however, there are merits in the church adopting any approach that would strengthen the governance/administration of its operations. Church leaders should, therefore, keep the governance structure simple and clear enough so that it can be followed and monitored effectively. With this in mind, we can concur with Harrington and Bertin that governance is based on three cornerstone principles of ownership, stewardship, and accountability. Using this as a guide, the objective of a simple and clear governance model can be devised.

SUMMARY OF GUIDELINES

1) Good corporate governance/administration helps to minimize scandals, misappropriation of funds, and corruptions.

2) People are more willing to invest in an organization that has a good governance structure, as this enhances trust.

3) Corporate governance is a relationship between church leaders, the church board, members, and other stakeholders, e.g., regulators and external partners.

4) Ensure the church has a clear mission and strategy and that these and the organization are well managed.

5) Do not operate with a tunnel view, because the church is impacted by political, cultural, social, and economic factors.

6) There are different systems of governance structures; the church must be mindful of this when crafting its governance structure.

7) Assess having a board of internal directors versus a mixed board of internal and external directors. The latter may be more effective, leading to more objectivity and trust.

CHAPTER 3
REGISTRATION OF CHURCH

"No matter how many mistakes you make or how slow you progress, you are still way ahead of everyone who isn't trying."

~ Anthony Robbins

Registration is an important requirement for businesses in Jamaica. Churches must be incorporated in accordance with the Companies Act, 2004, and are required to be registered with the Companies Office of Jamaica to be considered a legal entity. Churches or an arm of the church can also register under the charity's status with the Department of Cooperatives and Friendly Societies, but this would be based on the mission of the church.

Given the importance of the Companies Act, 2004, let us look at it in more details. The Companies Office of Jamaica, a regulatory body for businesses, monitors its members using the Companies Act, 2004. Hayle (2010) highlighted the definition for a small company in Jamaica as set out in the Companies Act, 2004, on the seventh schedule, part II. Small and medium-sized enterprises (SME) are defined as companies that meet two or more of the criteria specified in paragraph seven, which are: its turnover is less than $40 million; its balance sheet total is less than $30 million; and the total number of employees is less than 25. A holding company and its subsidiaries qualify as a small group in relation to a financial year if they meet, on a consolidated basis, two or more of the following criteria for that financial year and the financial years immediately preceding.

The criteria for small groups are: the group's turnover is less than $80 million; the balance sheet total is less than $60 million; and the total number of employees is less than 50. This guide is useful in looking at the size of the church as the regulator would assess size based on turnover, the dollar value of the balance sheet, and the number of employees. The size would determine whether the church is exempt from certain provisions, such as submitting annual audited accounts. However, based on the details of the act, a small church is not subjected to less regulation than a large church; they are both regulated in a similar fashion.

Most small churches in Jamaica comfortably meet the criteria above. However, the dissertation did not assess the size of churches on financial terms but instead on the size of membership. The Companies Act, 2004, is a critical document that shapes the operation of the organization and must be used by churches to ensure effective operation and compliance, as it includes provisions aimed at fostering good corporate governance (Kerr, 2005). Many people hope this would help to provide greater accountability by directors and fiduciaries of both public and private enterprises (Kerr, 2005). As Jamaican churches strive for good corporate governance, being registered with the Companies Office of Jamaica is one step in the right direction.

The following are some of the major forms used for registering a church and for ongoing reporting relationship with the Companies Office of Jamaica:

- Articles of Incorporation, Form 1B – This must be supported by Schedule 1 (which lists the Objectives and Powers and the Restrictions of the church) and Schedule 2.

- Declaration of Compliance, Form 2.
- Notice of Address of Registered Office or Notice of Change of Address of Registered Office, Form 17.
- Annual return, Company not having a share capital, Form 19B.
- Notice of Appointment or/Change of Company Secretary, Form 20.
- Notice of Appointment of/Change of Company Directors, Form 23.

For other types of businesses, similar forms are used, so one must be mindful of the forms that relate to its business. However, the Companies Office of Jamaica charges a fee for services rendered. The respective forms must be filled out and the payment made at the cashier. Once the registration is complete, the Companies Office of Jamaica will subsequently issue the church or business a Certificate of Incorporation. This clearly shows the registration status of the organization and the effective date it is registered.

At the point of registration, the church can use either of two options:

1) Register the church at the Companies Office of Jamaica with Limited on the church name and then request from the Ministry of Industry, Commerce, Agriculture and Fisheries the removal of the Limited, or

2) Request permission from the Ministry of Industry, Commerce, Agriculture and Fisheries to register the church without Limited on its name, then go to the Companies Office of Jamaica to start the registration process. Both options take time; therefore, the church must explore which is best at the time of registering.

For the removal of "Limited" from the church name, a letter must be written to the Ministry of Industry, Commerce, Agriculture and Fisheries to request this change. The letter will include the Company number and a copy of the Certificate of Incorporation, and the Articles of Incorporation must also be attached to this letter. A notice of this change must be published twice in newspapers, and subsequently, copies of these must be sent to the Ministry of Industry, Commerce, Agriculture and Fisheries to confirm that the notice was published. Where "Limited" is not removed, the church is expected to pay taxation annually.

Considering this is a legal expectation, it is assumed that churches will consider this to be very important and also ensure that it complies. Six of the ten churches in the dissertation indicated that they are registered with the Companies Office of Jamaica and are current with their filing to the Companies Office of Jamaica. Two pastors are uncertain of their churches' registration status.

Nevertheless, all registered churches must submit a copy of its financial statement to the Companies Office of Jamaica annually. The annual return must also be submitted, which is on Form 19B. This document contains detailed information about the church, a list of directors and contact information for the directors, an indication of who is doing the filing, and verification of whether there has been a change in the directors or the registered office of the church. It also indicates the period for which the filing is being done and the last filing done.

Where a church operates without being registered, it is operating illegally and could lead to the church being in breach of the laws of the land, and that is not acceptable from a spiritual point of view. A church, which is expected to promote honesty and integrity, should not, on the other hand, be engaged in breaking the law. This is a criminal offense and can bring the church into disrepute.

Thus, where a church is not registered, it is imperative that the pastor addresses the issue immediately, as the church could be ordered closed until the registration or the breaches are resolved.

Biblically, the church is expected to be submissive to civil authorities, as shown in 1 Peter 2:13-17. The church is also expected to obey the laws of the Land, which includes paying taxes as evidenced in Romans 13:1-14. As such, the church should obey man's law as God's law. Where this is not done, the person is rebelling not against man, but against God.

Furthermore, pastors are to ensure that the church has an effective strategy on how to foster and support continuity, as Searchy and Thomas (2006) purported that lack of strategy will limit the church's growth. With this in mind, the church must operate sensibly, ensuring that it is compliant. Therefore, the strategies employed must cover the business aspect of the church, which would be to generate money and record how it is used and also the spiritual aspect, which would be membership growth and the spiritual growth of the members.

McCahery and Vermeulen (2010) noted that the company law systems across jurisdictions contain rules on management control, disclosure, and transparency, which are designed to enable shareholders to employ legal techniques that secure accurate and timely information on the financial affairs and performance of the company. In general, company law also provides for basic techniques that protect minority shareholders' interests through participation rights and legal restrictions on managers' power to act in response to directions given by controlling shareholders. While this applies to business in general, it may not relate to the church, as it is registered as a Company not having a share capital.

Summary of Guidelines

1) Ensure the church is properly registered with the Companies Office of Jamaica and/or the Department of Cooperatives and Friendly Societies.

2) Ensure annual returns are made, providing accurate information at all times.

3) Compile the Incomes and Expenditures (Financial Statement) on an ongoing basis so that it can be filed along with the Annual Return.

4) Ensure the correct forms are used at all times and report changes of director, etc. in a timely manner.

5) Keep up to date on changes being made by the Companies Office of Jamaica and, in particular, any pronouncement by the government that would affect the regulatory requirements of the church.

6) The Annual Report is due based on the anniversary date of the registration. Ensure the returns are made on time and the associated fees are paid as well to avoid penalties.

STATUTORY OBLIGATION

"Time is more valuable than money. You can get more money, but you cannot get more time."

~ Jim Rohn

In dealing with statutory obligation, only one of the ten churches were required to file statutory returns, such as Pay As You Earn (PAYE), National Housing Trust (NHT), National Insurance Scheme (NIS), Human Employment and Resource Training (HEART), and Education Tax (Ed Tax), and these filings were current.

Most of the churches assessed were not liable for statutory returns. Notwithstanding, it is important to note that where the church employs individuals and pays a salary, the church will be required to make statutory returns.

For churches filing statutory returns, care should be exercised to ensure the returns are filed within the expected timelines. It is important that the calculations are properly done. There should also be a competent person in place to calculate and make the returns on time.

Church administrators must always keep abreast of changes being made by the government to its fiscal policies in the annual budget debate. The changes usually include property tax, general consumption tax, and taxes on emoluments, as previously mentioned.

Statutory returns or payment of taxes are expected within a specific time. For the statutory payments relating to emoluments, these must be paid by the 14th of each month for the previous month's statutory deductions. The deadline for the annual return is usually the 14th of March of each year for the calendar year preceding this date. That means the annual report for 2018 is due by March 14, 2019. Bear in mind, the government will issue correspondence on the changes to the deadline as it sees fit.

In my professional experience, I have seen where an additional amount had to be paid after year-end for statutory deductions. The main reason for this is that there are discrepancies between the monthly returns and the annual returns.

For property tax, these are due and payable by the 1st of April each year, covering the period of April to March in the following year. Therefore, the property tax paid on April 1, 2018 is for the fiscal year 2018/19 and would cover the period of April 1, 2018 to March 31, 2019. Currently, where the property tax is not paid on time, the penalty for late payment would come into effect within a specific time, and the penalty will continue to grow. Bear in mind, all landowners, including the church, are expected to pay property tax. There are some waivers available to churches, as it relates to the place of worship and land use for burial. The onus is on the church to ascertain its entitlement and make use of this benefit.

General Consumption Tax (GCT) is a crucial tax, which has a heavy penalty and interest attached to late or non-payment. Returns are expected to be filed, even when tax payable is nil. For nil returns, a flat rate is paid when submitting. The government determines how this impacts the consumer, and so there are ongoing changes to its administration. Currently, the church holds a zero-rated status. Zero-rated status means the church is not subjected to GCT. However, to enjoy this benefit, the church must do the following:

- Get an invoice for things being purchased.
- Take the invoice to the tax office to have it stamped.
- Then go to the vendor and make the purchase.
- The vendor will collect for the item(s) without charging the GCT, once the waiver stamp is affixed to the invoice.

For information, there is a mandatory limit of JA$3,000,000.00 for an organisation to be registered for GCT collection. Therefore, once the inflow for a 12-month period is expected to be JA$3M, the business can register. Registered organizations are required to file GCT returns by the last day of the month for the previous month. Therefore, the GCT Return for August 2018 is due on September 30, 2018. Where the last day of the month falls on a Saturday or Sunday, an effort must be made to pay by the Friday before those days. In some cases, the government may extend the deadline to Monday, considering the tax offices don't generally open on those days.

The church administrator must monitor extensions, but I recommend not relying on extensions. Furthermore, on the last day of the month, the tax office is generally full, as most taxpayers wait until the last day. Instead, church administrators should always pay taxes or make returns early, that is, before the due date. Incidentally, where the payment is late, you are subjected to the penalty or interest, and excuses are usually not accepted. Failure to pay the interest and penalty on time will cause more charges to be incurred, as the penalty and interest on outstanding GCT are charged on a daily basis.

I have witnessed payments for GCT being made late because the tax office was full, and the bearer eventually did not get in to make the payment. As such, penalty and interest had to be paid. Furthermore, one must check all receipts to ensure they are correct because the tax system will generate a notice at later dates for late or non-payment.

Generally, these notices are mailed to the organizations they relate to and are sent out months after the action took place, sometimes up to six months.

Where the organization cannot prove that it was an error made by the tax office, that organization will have to pay the penalty and interest. Incidentally, this could be six months of penalty and interest, which could be a tidy sum, especially where the organization has large balances. Therefore, issues concerning the GCT must be monitored carefully.

Tax computation is vital because where short payment is made due to errors in the calculation or lack of knowledge about changes made by the government, interest and penalties could be incurred on the outstanding amounts.

The church should also keep informed on any waivers or other benefits that are available to the church, as these could be helpful to a church struggling financially. Failure to claim a waiver or benefit could be a lost opportunity, as they could be time sensitive or tied to specific activities, which, if not done within the expected time or while the activities are taking place, may be lost forever.

The government over the years continues to make an improvement to tax collection. Currently, most tax-related transactions can be done online. However, for proper recordkeeping, church administrators must ensure that this is monitored properly. In some cases, after a payment is made online, you are expected to subsequently request the official receipt from the tax office. Over time, I expect this to improve.

Overall, church administrators must always assess which tax applies to the church and deal with them appropriately. Likewise, administrators must keep abreast of possible waivers and benefits. All of these forms a part of good governance.

Summary of Guidelines

1) Once people are employed by the church, it is expected that the church will make statutory returns. The statutory returns for taxes on emolument are PAYE, NHT, NIS, HEART, and Ed Tax. Other taxes the church may have to pay are Business Tax, GCT, and Property Tax. The leaders are to ascertain the taxes relevant to the church and monitor the payments.

2) Ensure filings are done on time. Taxes on emolument are due by the 14th of each month for the previous month. A monthly return and an annual return in March of each year for the previous year is expected, using the calendar year (January to December). Business Tax is due twice per year, June and September, but can be paid once in full. GCT is due the last working day of the month for the previous month. Property Tax is due on the 1st of April each year.

3) Penalty and interest are applicable to some of these taxes. Be current on how to accurately calculate these taxes. Where the calculation is incorrect, a penalty could eventually be applied.

4) Keep abreast of changes being made by the government regarding these taxes. Ignorance is no excuse under the law. The government generally makes the changes during the annual budget debate, which is done in the first half of each year.

5) In addition to assessing which taxes are applicable, one should also assess the waivers and financial benefits available to the church.

6) Check receipts for tax payments made to ensure the correct information is presented. This will avoid the time it takes to appeal or seek corrections.

Codes of Best Practices

"It is the mark of an educated mind to be able to entertain a thought without accepting it."

~ Aristotle

Harrington and Bertin (2009) indicated that corporate governance codes of best practice are sets of nonbinding recommendations aimed at improving and guiding the governance practices of corporations within a country's specific legal environment and business context. In addition, the following definitions were retrieved from the internet:

> ***A code of practice*** *is a set of professional standards or written guidelines agreed on by members of a particular profession or written guidelines issued*

by an official body or a professional association to its members to help them comply with its ethical standards. Codes of Practice set out industry standards of conduct. They are guidelines for fair dealing between you and your customers, and let your customers know what your business agrees to do when dealing with them. Codes of Practice can relate to a single business or represent a whole industry.

A **best practice** is a technique or methodology that, through experience and research, has proven to reliably lead to the desired result. A commitment to using the best practices in any field is a commitment to using all the knowledge and technology at one's disposal to ensure success. A best practice is a method or technique that has consistently shown results superior to those achieved with other means, and that is used as a benchmark.

A **code of conduct** is a set of rules outlining the social norms and rules and responsibilities of, or proper practices for, an individual, party, or organization. Related concepts include ethical, honor, moral codes and religious laws.

A **code of ethics** document may outline the mission and values of the business or organization, how professionals are supposed to approach problems, *the ethical principles based on the organization's core values and the standards to which the professional is held. A code of ethics is usually established by a professional order to protect the public and the reputation of the professionals. Indeed, people who breach their code of ethics incur disciplinary actions that can range from a warning or reprimand to dismissal or expulsion from their professional order.*

The terms "Code of Ethics" and "Code of Conduct" are often mistakenly used interchangeably. They are, in fact, two unique documents. Codes of ethics, which govern decision-making, and codes of conduct, which govern actions, represent two common ways that companies self-regulate.

A code of professional conduct *is a necessary component for any profession to maintain standards for the individuals within that profession to adhere. It brings about accountability, responsibility, and trust to the individuals that the profession serves.*

As the organization crafts its codes of best practice, the information from the internet could be helpful in that process. This covers code of practice, code of conduct, code of ethics, and code of professional conduct. These will guide the leaders' decisions and behavior. They will also guide the behavior of the entire organization.

Codes of best practice speak to the most effective or efficient method of achieving an objective or completing a task. Harrington and Bertin presented ten global corporate governance drivers. One of these drivers is that there are many success stories proving that the use of corporate governance best practices and a professional Board of Directors are good for business, not only in major companies but also with smaller and family-owned businesses.

The main objective of a company code of best practices is to suggest courses of action that will improve the company's performance and facilitate access to capital (Harrington & Bertin, 2009). One important factor that the codes of best practices should include as it seeks to improve and maintain performance is succession planning – a plan for future replacement of personnel. As such, Succession Planning will be dealt with in Chapter 8.

Codes of best practice are important for the organization because with it, the organization will not operate in isolation. It will use procedures and recommendations that are tested and utilized in the other context. When implementing the codes of best practice, one should aim to bring improvements to the organization. With these non-binding recommendations, it means the organization would have the freedom to change or modify whatever recommendation is not working. Where there is a long-term plan, such as the acquisition of major assets, the codes of best practice will set the organization on the right path to obtain financial assistance, such as a loan or an investment.

SUMMARY OF GUIDELINES

1) The church can benefit from the experience and wisdom of others by developing codes of best practices.

2) Explore what is obtained at other churches, reviewing about five churches, to help in developing what will govern your church.

3) Discuss among leaders and members what is relevant and workable for your church.

4) Have a compiled document with all the codes of best practices.

5) Review these codes periodically at least every three to five years.

CHAPTER 6
ADMINISTRATION

"Answer these questions often: What are you doing? Why are you doing it? Where is this going?"

~ Jed McKenna

Administration is the art and science of planning, organizing, leading, and controlling the work of others to achieve defined objectives and goals (Welsh, 2011). For administration to work in the local church or any religious non-profit organization, Welsh noted that long-held misconceptions must be dealt with.

Welsh presented some often-stated objections to administration in the church. Four of these objections are: firstly, the church is a spiritual environment and should not have a business atmosphere. Secondly, administration is an unspiritual activity and has little to do with the ecclesiastical processes and ministry of the church. Thirdly, administration takes a minister (or a leader) out of their primary role and places him in a position where he becomes a "desk jockey" or having his ministry controlled by a group of Boards or Committees. Finally, the church is fit together by the Holy Spirit and needs no human help or intervention.

In addition to its spiritual focus, the church has administrative duties that must be performed. In many instances, not much attention is given to this important area, perhaps due to the misconceptions raised by Welsh. Notwithstanding, Crandall (1995) stated that one of the gifts and skills for ministry is administration and organization. Even if the pastor is not personally doing the administrative work, the pastor must oversee it and ensure it is done properly.

Concerning the issue of administration, Byassee (2010) posited that big churches can take care of themselves. The problem is with denominational officials, pastors, and laypeople thinking their small church should be big and are made to (or make themselves) feel like failures when it doesn't happen. O'Brien (2010) speaks to what a small church can do when it stops thinking of itself as a failed effort to get big and starts capitalizing on its unique strengths. Patterson (1992) noted that when we view the church as a religious organization representing God's interests on earth, we will naturally view church leaders as administrators and managers.

Stevens (1967) indicated that Church administration may be designated by the terms church government, church polity, church order, church organization, or church constitution. He also indicated that every group of believers in Christ calling itself a church has some form of government. These forms are generally classified as: monarchical, Episcopal, Presbyterian, and congregational. Patterson (1992) only promotes three of these forms of church government, namely, Episcopal, Presbyterian, and congregational. Regardless of the size or structure of the church, there will be administrative work to be done. No wonder it's one of the giftings of the Holy Spirit. Where administration is not under control, one could assume the church lacks this gifting.

Tyson (2007) looked at the biblical understanding of administration and leadership. The spiritual gifts, as evident in 1 Corinthians 12, Romans 12, and Ephesians 4, are given to all Christians, not just the ordained. The gifts are necessary for the healthy functioning of the body of Christ. Tyson (2007) stated that since each of us has some of the gifts, and none of us has all of them, we must band together and share our mutual gifted-ness to create a fully functioning body. Tyson also shows that spiritual gifts are given to us graciously by God to carry out the ministries to which He called us.

Tyson (2007) encouraged pastors to earnestly desire the spiritual gifts of administration and leadership because it is very difficult to be an effective pastor without them. He believes administration and leadership are interconnected and that the words are used interchangeably in Scripture, in pastoral teaching, and in the secular world. Although the words administration and leadership are being used interchangeably, there are some important aspects to consider about leadership, and this will be dealt with in a separate Chapter.

Financial administration is crucial; therefore, managing the finances of the church is a critical area and must be considered in a corporate governance structure (Elson et al. 2006). There is a need for strong budgetary controls, wise spending patterns, and successful long-term investment strategies.

Some churches engage the role of a treasurer to manage the financial arm of the church. However, I strongly recommend that the financial status of the church must be an agenda item of the Board Meetings to ensure the Board gives oversight to the status of the church's finances.

Tyson believes pastors should never handle the church's cash at any time but should ensure, through the finance committee, that policies are set and followed for the proper handling of money. He emphasized the need for money to be counted and deposited, and that statements should be issued annually to members. This is in an effort to create an environment of transparency and accountability. Tyson concluded that irregularity or scandal in the realm of finances can destroy a congregation or a pastor's ministry. He also indicated that observing due diligence with church finance is not difficult or complicated, but it is vital.

Capaldi (2005) posited that we call corporate governance the application of the fiduciary principle to the management of corporations. He further pointed out that the fiduciary duties of corporate directors and officers have their origin in principles of natural law. However, corporate governance scandals over the past decade reflected a widespread failure to adhere to the traditional duties of good faith, loyalty, and care.

Fiduciary duties are part of the contractual nature of the corporation and exist to fill in the blanks and inevitable oversights in the actual contracts used by business organizations (Macey, 2011). The purpose of fiduciary duties is to provide people with the results that they would have bargained for if they had been able to anticipate the problem at hand and had contracted for its resolution in advance. In addition to how the church would govern its finances, there are some expectations and requirements in the Companies Act, 2004, that must be considered as part of managing the sustainability of the church in Jamaica.

My view is that administration ensures things are under control, which includes smooth operational flow, processes being completed on time, reports being prepared in a timely manner, payments made on time, and all issues regarding compliance with regulators and statutory obligations are met.

Most administrative work for a church is usually done outside of regular service times. Therefore, in some cases, someone with the requisite skills should be engaged or employed to do these tasks efficiently. Small churches may struggle to pay a person to do the administrative work of the church. However, the members must be informed of the importance of this area of responsibility. Where people in the church have this skill, voluntary work could be done among a group of people to share the workload and ensure the church maintains effective administrative control.

The administrative role is carried out in all types and forms of business, especially the management of human resources. The church has to deal with human resource management but to a lesser extent. The church must prepare letters for members, sign official documents, facilitate meetings to address conflicts between members, and plan training sessions to improve the members spiritually, especially in areas where there is an obvious deficiency.

Administration is a God-given, motivational, spiritual gift that can be developed (See 1 Corinthians 12:28). It involves the ability to rule in the church and govern the things of God. Administrators of the church are expected to be shepherds, promoting order in the body of Christ.

Summary of Guidelines

1) Churches must be mindful that good administration is crucial, and it is one gifting of the Holy Spirit.

2) Financial Administration is an important area; it can make or break the church. This includes managing the inflows and outflows and should be an agenda item for all Board meetings.

3) Human Resource Management is an area that the church must pay attention to. The members are to be developed and monitored.

4) Pastors should not attempt to carry the administrative role alone but should seek paid people or volunteers to help in the work.

5) Administration involves taking charge of all legal, regulatory, and operational issues at all times. This also involves ensuring things are in order and making notes at all times rather than relying on memory.

CHAPTER 7
LEADERSHIP AND STRATEGIC PLANNING

"We seem to gain wisdom more readily through our failures than through our successes. We always think of failure as the antithesis of success, but it isn't. Success often lies just on the other side of failure."

~ Leo Buscaglia

The leadership of the organization is an important tool, as it helps in continuity, achieving objectives, facilitates proper control over day-to-day operations, and can lead to growth in the membership. Good leadership steers an organization in a positive and productive direction. Good leadership will help minimize problems by being proactive in its operation. However, where problems arise, good leadership will exercise problem-solving skills and damage control.

Dudley (2003) gives three categories of leadership, as follows:

- <u>Associational (traditional) leadership</u> – provides effective guidance for gathering membership with a free commitment to the mission of the church.
- <u>Organizational (rational) leadership</u> – provides careful, efficient administration. They are the easiest to find and often find you first, with an agenda in one hand and a calendar in the other. They manage the church events.
- <u>Spiritual (charismatic) leadership</u> – helps people know themselves through the eyes of faith.

Embracing all three leadership tasks – traditional, relational, and charismatic – may be heavy, but pastors should at least be sensitive to the variety of characters in the congregation and to the various roles they contribute to reaching a congregational decision (Dudley, 2003).

Leadership can be in the form of the pastor, the Board, or the department heads. Leadership in the church is just as critical as leadership in the business organization. Channon (1999) noted that the role of the Chief Executive Officer and/or Chairman is critical in establishing corporate strategy, culture, and direction. A major shift in the corporate strategy, culture, and direction of a company usually only occurs after a change in one or both of these senior officers.

Interestingly, Bickers (2005) revealed that poor leadership from both the pastor and lay preacher can severely limit a church's effectiveness. He further stated that some common possible causes of conflict in a church are stress, pride, fear, and poor leadership. Leaders need to be mindful of this to minimize the possible conflicts and foster a better ongoing relationship between leaders and members.

Not all details of church governance are plainly taught or implied by Scripture (Swartley, 2005). Leadership, therefore, must use its best judgment, informed by the general teaching of the Word, while being careful to preserve the functions and essential character of the New Testament church. Swartley (2005) noted that Jesus taught

His disciples to function collectively, not as individuals, as He led them to work together as a group, sent them by twos to preach, and instructed them to remain together until Pentecost. Welsh (2011) validated the scriptural necessity of efficient church administration but also provided the leadership and administrators with effective tools to meet the mission and purpose of their church or organization.

Daman (2008) mentioned that a small church is different from its larger counterpart, as it views leadership differently. He stated that often, leaders mistakenly assume the principles of leadership and ministry operate the same, regardless of church size. Daman (2008) revealed that leadership needs to be convinced that the vision is both possible and essential. If the leaders do not believe in the vision, neither will the people. He further stated that articulating the vision requires the leadership to explain how it will affect the lives of the people involved in the ministry. This suggests to me that a major part of leadership is communication. Having a good vision without being able to communicate that vision could result in the membership not being empowered to support that vision, hence the vision could die or there could be major challenges in carrying it out.

Kreider (2008) also shared a critical view, stating that leaders in both the Old and New Testaments did not work alone but with a team of leaders who served with them. It is said that "teamwork makes the dream work," and I endorse the teamwork approach among leaders. Among a team is a wider collection of skills, knowledge, and expertise, which supersede what one individual of the leadership team would have. Furthermore, with a united force, greater achievement can be realized.

Osborne (2008) posited that every organization eventually becomes a direct reflection of its leadership, whether for good or for bad. This clearly shows that leadership must lead by example and model the behavior and vision it expects of the organization. Smaller churches can develop better leaders because the smaller the congregation, the greater the opportunity for children to be active leaders (Chronmey, 1995). Along with demonstrated gifts of leadership, one must possess extraordinary interpersonal skills (Waltz, 2005). Interpersonal skills will assist in sharing the strategy with the team.

Searcy and Thomas (2006) emphasize that a lack of strategy will limit your church growth. This, therefore, speaks to the importance of strategic planning and strategic leadership. To promote the degree of strategic leadership, five qualifications, among others, are necessary (Caver, 2006). These qualification areas are as follows:

- Commitment to the ownership and to the organization's specific area of endeavor.
- Propensity for thinking in terms of systems and context.
- Ability and eagerness to deal with values, vision, and the long-term.
- Ability to participate assertively in deliberation.
- Willingness to delegate, to allow others to make decisions.

Strategic planning is a critical leadership quality. In looking at the concept of strategic planning in business, McKenna and Beech (2002) shared the following three generally agreed-on facets of strategy:

- Strategy affects the overall direction and potential for success of the organization.
- Strategy is concerned with the fit between the environment and the organization.
- Strategy deals with non-routine activities and is seeking innovation and change in the organization.

McKenna and Beech (2002) also stated that business strategy is concerned with the efficient use of resources, as well as ensuring that the mobilization of those resources achieves the maximum impact.

As we focus on the efficient use of resources, managing finance is a crucial part of this process. Financial Management will determine the outcomes and the maximum impact that will be realized. With good strategic planning, money should not be spent carelessly, but in a sensible manner. This will ensure value for money, that only what is really needed will be purchased, and that items required are procured in a timely manner.

Under normal circumstances, members may not share the vision of the leaders, but with careful planning and clear direction, the members will be in a better position to support its leaders. This will foster the opportunity for the organization to collectively achieve its goals. Overall, strategic planning will chart the long-term direction of the organization. It will develop and maintain the policies and procedures to guide the organization. The leaders at the strategic level will delegate and communicate the strategies so they can be followed by people at the operational and tactical level.

SUMMARY OF GUIDELINES

1) Leadership is essential for continuity, good administration, and growth.

2) Good leadership steers an organization in a positive and productive direction and helps minimize problems by being proactive.

3) One leader may not possess all categories of leadership, so assessing the talents available to the church is advisable, and it is important to utilize those talents through a team effort. This will help foster good leadership.

4) Strategy, culture, and direction are established and maintained by the leaders, including senior officers and board members.

5) It is advisable that a leader does not operate as a one-man show, as it can result in being burnt out, overworked, and ineffective. Jesus usually sent His disciples in pairs for their mission, which is an example for us. There are merits in differences of opinion, style, and knowledge.

6) The principles of leadership and ministry will vary based on the size of the church. Leaders are to function based on their reality and not what other churches are able to do. Notwithstanding, they should be prepared to challenge themselves.

CHAPTER 8
SUCCESSION PLANNING

"Set goals that make you feel powerful, motivated, and driven when you focus on them."

~ Steve Pavlina

Succession planning is an ideal approach to ensure that the organization continues when senior leaders are terminated. This planning is imperative, as the future can have many uncertainties, and unforeseen circumstances can arise. This is a proactive approach to dealing with eventualities that may arise. McKenna and Beech (2002) stated that succession planning calls for an assessment of the actual performance of the people in their positions, with their potential for promotion firmly in mind. This usually entails a formal plan to broaden the individual's knowledge and experience of many aspects of work in a particular area and/or training in skills at the technical and human relations level. These authors encourage leaders to guard against the misuse of succession planning where it is seen as a means of placing certain groups at a disadvantage.

Hayle (2010) defines succession planning as a process for identifying and developing internal people with the potential to fill key leadership positions in the company. This increases the availability of experienced and capable employees that are prepared to assume these roles as they become available. Taken narrowly, 'replacement planning' for key roles is the heart of succession planning. Effective succession planning or talent-pool management concerns itself with building a series of feeder groups up and down the entire leadership pipeline or progression (Charan, Drotter, & Noel, 2001). In contrast, replacement planning is focused narrowly on identifying specific backup candidates for given senior management positions.

McLachlan (2005) revealed that there are hard-set rules about succession planning for the election of a new Pope. He showed that over the years, the Pope in power would make changes as they saw fit.

In 1996, Pope John Paul 11 promulgated a whole new set of rules in the Constitution. This means succession follows a particular process. On the contrary, Beech (2011) reported that in China, at the age of 76 years old, the 14th Dalai Lama, the Tibetan spiritual leader, promised clear succession guidelines to be given when he is around 90 years old. Subsequently, he raised intriguing possibilities in his statements, that his reincarnation could be chosen before he died, and that the line would end with him, meaning there would be no 15th Dalai Lama. This certainly conflicts with the secular policy of succession planning. As leaders make succession plans, it is also necessary to make decisions. Quite often, the candidate(s) selected for promotion will need further training and development. A decision must be made regarding this and other matters of the organization.

All the pastors in the study held the view that the church would continue effectively if he or she relinquished his or her position. This view was expressed even where they indicated that no system was in place to guarantee this effective continuity.

The systems in place for those churches that have given attention to this issue include the sharing of information and the training of prospective successors. These systems should be promoted among all the churches, as they seem appropriate and will encourage sustainability and continuity. This study motivated one of the pastors, who now intends to have a dialogue with the overseer so that these systems can be implemented in that particular church.

It can be challenging when a leader is leaving or is to be promoted and no one is prepared to take over that vacant role. When my pastor died suddenly, we all realized no one was adequately prepared for her position, as there was no succession plan in place. The church was like a fish out of water. We did not know where we were going or how to get there. This was the main motivation behind doing the dissertation and, ultimately, this book, because as a church, some critical issues were not being attended to over the years.

We had to hold meetings, using leaders from other churches to guide us and help us get on our feet. This included interviewing people for ordination and conducting the ordination ceremony of new leaders. At this point, we had to appoint and ordain a team of people to champion the work. In the past, people would give support to the pastorate, because they were officially appointed as lay ministers. However, there was no clear strategy as to who would succeed the pastor. Furthermore, the lay ministers were not privy to all the matters concerning the church, only the areas he or she had to deal with.

One good thing in our case is that people had gone to Bible School and Seminary on their own, not by the church's request. Those who were appointed had the requisite biblical training and ability to effectively fill roles that were now vacant or created. Consider the situation the church would be in if no one was trained or prepared in this way. The challenges would have been much greater for the church to move forward. In cases like these, the members could have left for other churches. We also experienced a few people leaving, but most returned later when they saw that we were on our feet. It is said that "failure to plan means that we plan to fail." With that in mind, churches must be encouraged to take the whole business of succession planning seriously, as this leads to a smooth operational flow when an unforeseen situation arises, resulting in a leader not being able to continue in his or her present role.

Although we have overcome some aspects, some areas remain a challenge. The people have been accustomed to things being done a particular way for over 60 years. As such, some people could not come to grips with a leader younger than themselves. Some people began to push their own agenda by trying to change rules they had wanted to see changed for a long time. Consequently, it took time to iron out the various issues while the healing and grieving process was taking place.

The main systems in place, as indicated by the pastor in the study, could be followed. However, it was clear that some pastors had no plan at all. With this in mind, church leaders must ensure there is communication of the strategy, people are appointed and trained to fill roles, and, most importantly, I recommend that people be given a chance to act in the role before the official person is removed from the role. The general membership must be informed that this is the direction so that if something happens suddenly, it does not send shock waves to the operation of the organization. This could reduce rebellion and the kinds of challenges that come when there is any form of disagreement or conflict.

SUMMARY OF GUIDELINES

1) Ensure people are being prepared/developed to take over from the present leaders. This calls for an assessment of people's suitability and capability for the respective positions.

2) Replacement planning for key roles is the heart of succession planning.

3) Succession planning can be classified as talent-pool management, where specific backup candidates are identified for given senior management positions.

4) It is ideal to meet with key people internally to develop succession planning, but outside help is also advisable.

5) There must be communication of the strategy to all. People are to be appointed and trained for the various roles. It is more important for the replacements to act in the role before key people leave the office.

Chapter 9

Accountability

"Let others lead small lives, but not you. Let others argue over small things, but not you. Let others cry over small hurts, but not you. Let others leave their future in someone else's hands, but not you."

~ Jim Rohn

Accountability has to do with responsibility. Therefore, a lack thereof can result in a breakdown within organizations, resulting in a loss of respect for the leaders. The church is not exempt from this situation. According to BD (2017), accountability is:

"the obligation of an individual or organization to account for its activities, accept responsibility for

> *them, and to disclose the results in a transparent manner. It also includes the responsibility for money or other entrusted property."*

Regarding how the church emphasizes accountability, a wide range of remarks emerged. The pastor is expected to be honest, trustworthy, transparent, and willing to share information; the Board members make decisions collectively; there are people in place serving as accountability partners; members are informed of decisions or changes; members are asked to give feedback; evaluation of the services and leadership is done by the members; procedure is given to people doing tasks; people are expected to do their best, to perform at a good standard and a high quality.

Regarding with whom accountability lies, the respondents gave mixed views. In one case, it was the secretary, while in three cases, it was everyone. In most cases (six out of ten), the pastors indicated that accountability lies with the leaders, which includes pastors, the bishop, officers, and Board members. Interestingly, one pastor stated that "Accountable Officers are expected to keep records current, safeguard items in their care, recognizing his/herself as a servant of God."

In another case, the pastor indicated that the secretary keeps records up-to-date, and, thus, accountability lies with the secretary.

The findings also show that some emphasis on accountability is evident, as each pastor shared their views on how this is achieved. The process involves focusing on the character of people, making information available, requesting feedback, conducting evaluations, and having standards of quality in place. These points, if applied correctly, will help small churches to act efficiently. However, the central concern lies in the issue of who accountability lies with. While it may be commendable that accountability is being placed on the leaders, people performing tasks must be encouraged to operate responsibly. This must be communicated to all so that there is no blame game when challenges arise, as each person would clearly know what is expected.

While it is understandable that the pastor cannot do everything himself or herself, the structures and systems must be in place for delegation and monitoring to take place at regular intervals. It is common for people to be given an area of responsibility for which they are not trained or skilled, thus being left alone to function on autopilot. In cases like these, sometimes it is only when something detrimental happens that accountability becomes important. However, with good corporate governance, accountability is always an important facet. As such, from the outset, the church must give clear attention to this.

With that said, accountability should not just be written on paper – it should be clearly communicated to all. When this is done, the Accountability Officer will know his/herself, and the entire organization will also know this person. It should never be when something goes wrong or there is a breach that a person is told that he or she was responsible. The Accountability Officer must know that he or she is the vanguard for the organization's assets and properties. With that in mind, every care must be given when performing his or her duty. At every level, proper due diligence must be followed, likewise strict attention should be given to the policies that govern the operations of the organization.

There have been cases where people were fired from the organization because they were negligent or for some other reason. However, the crucial thing is that sometimes the person was not adequately prepared for such tasks. Therefore, there must be a good reporting structure in place, and the organizational chart must be clear to all. People will know who they report to, who to take directives from, who to report problems to, who to seek intervention from, and who to seek additional resources from.

Incidentally, accountability covers recordkeeping, which includes financial and other documents. The person responsible for the finances must ensure approval is given before any payment is made. Likewise, all supporting documents should be in place and the proper procedures followed.

Accountability also involves the organization being compliant. Therefore, someone must monitor the timelines to ensure they are met. This includes the timelines for procuring resources, meeting tax and statutory obligations, training people to deal with changes, doing the day-to-day tasks on time and in the expected manner, communicating critical information within a reasonable time, making critical decisions, and setting and reviewing policies in a timely manner.

SUMMARY OF GUIDELINES

1) Accountability has to do with responsibility.

2) Although a church may see the leader as accountable, people performing tasks must be encouraged to operate responsibly.

3) Expectations must be communicated to all to avoid an unnecessary blame game when challenges arise.

4) Structures and systems must be in place for delegation and monitoring at regular intervals.

5) Ensure people are adequately trained for their areas of responsibility.

6) It should not be when something goes wrong or there is a breach for someone to know he/she was responsible.

7) The Accountability Officer is the vanguard for the organization's assets, properties, records, and compliance.

8) Care must be exercised when performing one's duty. Due diligence must be exercised and strict attention given to policies that govern the operations of the organization.

Recordkeeping

"Learn from yesterday, live for today, hope for tomorrow."

~ Albert Einstein

Recordkeeping is a crucial part of good governance. This involves proper systems to protect titles, certificates, receipts, and other documents, which could assist in justifying ownership or proving that particular transactions were done. Recordkeeping also involves preserving relevant historical information, including decisions made at meetings in the form of minutes and files. Storage of pertinent information about members or staff of the organization is crucial and must be held in strict confidence. Recording of financial transactions on a timely basis is also a huge part of good recordkeeping. Once a good recording of the financial transaction is in place, reports can be subsequently prepared. Storage of the financial reports is also essential, as it gives a picture of the organization's status at a particular point in time.

As it relates to financial records, it is commendable when churches are current with their financial reporting. The secretaries and/or pastors need to ensure that the records are maintained. I know of cases where the church's finances are in disarray, which speaks to a lack of accountability. When this happens, it could lead to assumptions which are not encouraging for the leaders or the church on the whole. People could also accuse the leader of stealing the church funds. Therefore, there must be transparency and proper systems in place to manage the movement of money in and out of the organization.

In the study, it was highlighted that Tyson (2007) advises pastors never to handle the church's cash at any time but should ensure through the finance committee that policies are set and followed for the proper handling of money. In Jamaica, pastors are commonly accused of living lavishly from the members' tithes and offerings. As part of best practice and to protect their integrity, pastors should adopt this guideline given by Tyson.

Furthermore, proper financial controls could include greater segregation of duties, for example, two people counting and recording the collections, with different people being assigned to deal with the lodgements. Assigning someone else to verify lodgement slips, and that the collection reports agree is also advisable. This person can also be responsible for authorizing the overall spending of the church funds.

In essence, basic accounting principles should be applied for good governance of the funds. The pastor could seek assistance from members who have accounting skills or employ someone to carry out the function. Where proper accounting is done, coupled with informative and accurate reports, the leaders will be empowered to make critical decisions. The reports will also show the status of the organization, which will help in silencing the critics or minimizing speculations.

As it relates to the status of the documentation that was reviewed, the researcher encouraged churches to ensure that proper storage systems are implemented at the church facilities. Having done that, at least two people should have access to those files so that in the event of unforeseen occurrences, the church can smoothly continue efficiently. The fact that one of the churches surveyed had a fire in the past and all its documents were destroyed is a lesson to the others to implement a fireproof storage facility to secure important documents.

It is important that the church maintains an office where documents for the church can be properly stored. All trustees should have access to the storage. Therefore, there should be a protocol or policy in place to manage this access by the trustees. With an office, there should be adequate filing cabinets, shelves, vaults, or a safe. These should be adequately secured with locks and keys or codes. Fire safety must be of paramount importance. Therefore, assistance can be sought from a fire protection company within Jamaica, so they can inspect and give their recommendations. They can recommend fire extinguishers to be installed in the office/storage areas. These fire extinguishers will have to be checked periodically to ensure they operate efficiently.

The volume of information and documents the church has will determine the level of storage required. This can be a simple filing system or an elaborate one. However, whatever the level of storage, someone must be accountable for this area. Where the filing is elaborate, perhaps people will have to be trained to manage it. They must be able to label, index, and code documents for filing so that the stored information can be located promptly in the future.

Consequently, recordkeeping is concerned with the storage of documents, reports, and files, but also the quality and security of the filing systems. The filing should also be done efficiently so that the information or documents can be easily retrieved when they are needed. People having custody of the keys to storage areas or vault codes must be confidential and trustworthy. The membership should feel comfortable that the information about themselves and the church, in general, are kept safely and privately. Recordkeeping is linked to the protection of assets. As such, in the next chapter, we will deal with the acquisition of assets.

SUMMARY OF GUIDELINES

1) Recordkeeping is important to prove ownership and to justify transactions. Recordkeeping also covers the security of the documents and information filed and the easy retrieval of those documents and information when needed.

2) Recordkeeping involves preserving relevant historical information, such as decisions made at meetings.

3) Confidentiality must govern the storage of information, especially information on the members and staff of the church.

4) Good recordkeeping also includes financial transactions and, ultimately, the financial reports.

5) A proper system must be in place to record the movement of money in and out of the organization.

6) Good accounting and accurate reports empower leaders to make critical decisions.

7) To facilitate good recordkeeping, proper storage must be in place, e.g., an office with a policy to govern access to this critical area. It should have adequate filing cabinets, shelves, a vault, a safe, and fireproof storage for important documents. Furthermore, fire safety is of paramount importance for the storage area(s).

8) The volume of information and documents will determine the level of storage needed, ranging from simple to elaborate.

9) People must be trained to manage the recordkeeping, and they must be trustworthy and accountable for this important area of the church.

Acquisition of Assets

*"Efficiency is doing things right;
effectiveness is doing the right things."*

~ Peter Drucker

The names used when purchasing assets were reviewed. Most of the major assets of the churches were purchased in the respective churches' names. Only two of the participating churches of this study rented or leased the places of worship, while in two other cases, there were negotiations to purchase the land the church is on. In another case, it was revealed that a lot of land was purchased in trustees' names before the church was registered and, presently, the three trustees are deceased (at the time of the research only two of the trustees were deceased).

Two of the properties that the churches are built on belong to the respective pastors, who are the legitimate owners. In one case, a former member donated the land to the church. That person is now deceased, and the land was not transferred to the church.

It is important to bear in mind that the ownership of properties is only confirmed by the churches' names being on the land titles. Furthermore, where the trustees are deceased, this needs to be addressed expeditiously because the land could become the property of the state (crown land), and it can be challenging for the church to reclaim ownership. In fact, family members can make claims on the land and demand compensation on the grounds that the property belongs to their family and not the church.

A procurement policy is of paramount importance and should cover the following:

- The tendering process, which should be dependent on the kind of assets being purchased.
- The approval process, with a clear indication of the Accountability Officer.
- Guidelines on selecting vendors, which must always be a legal source.

- Details regarding how decisions are made, which should cover getting the best quality at the most reasonable price.

A financial policy regarding the acquisition of assets is also important, as this will guide the decisions of the person(s) responsible for carrying out or supporting the process for the procurement of the assets. This financial policy should cover the following:

- The financial limits.
- The Accountability Officers.
- Guidelines on the disbursement of funds, especially where deposits must be made long before the asset is received.
- The organization's stance on how to finance the purchase of major assets, such as through borrowing, leasing, or outright cash.

Safeguarding of the assets acquired is a crucial matter that all churches must pay attention to. This includes maintaining a fixed asset register, which will track the following:

- Date of purchase
- Details of the payment and the cost price

- The name of the vendor
- The location in which the asset is placed
- The depreciation rates
- Identification numbers, such as serial number or manufacturer number

The physical asset should also be labeled so it can be clearly identified. In this case, similar items such as chairs would be assigned a number to distinguish each separately. Details of the label placed on the assets or number assigned must be noted on the fixed asset register.

A location listing can also be placed in each area, which will list all the assets in that location. Periodically, the location listing should be checked against the physical assets to identify whether anything is missing. The people who do the inspection should note on the listing the date of inspection and sign off on the form. A transfer listing should be in place to note the movement of assets from one location to the next. Where an asset will permanently be removed, the location listing should be updated.

The storage of documents is covered in Chapter 10, which deals with recordkeeping. Suffice it to say, documentation is important in a court case. In the study, there were concerns about the storage of important documents, including those relating to the procurement of assets. The main concern is that the documents are being stored at the pastors'/secretaries' homes due to the churches not having offices. This is a serious issue, as there is the possibility of the churches' documents being mislaid or not being accounted for. This includes financial records and members' personal details, which can lead to confidentiality issues or identity theft issues. When the pastor or secretary migrates or dies, retrieving documents that were not handed over may be impossible. Therefore, all documents regarding assets purchased and the ownership of the assets must be stored properly.

SUMMARY OF GUIDELINES

1) Ensure the properties of the church are purchased in the church's name and not in the names of leaders or trustees. This must be evidenced on all receipts and titles.

2) Ensure titles and receipts are properly filed/stored (see Chapter 10 for details)

3) Implement a procurement policy, which covers the tendering process, approval process, guidelines on selecting legal vendors, and details of how decisions are made. Always ensure you get the best quality at the most reasonable price.

4) A financial policy is also good, as it supports the procurement policy. This covers limits, the Accountability Officer, guidelines on disbursement of funds, and guidance on the purchase of major assets.

5) Safeguard the assets using a fixed asset register, which should track the date of purchase, details of the items, cost, names of vendors, location of the assets, depreciation rate, depreciation charge, serial/model numbers, and identification numbers established by the organization.

6) Label all assets individually using alphanumeric codes. This distinguishing code must be on the fixed asset register.

7) A location listing should be placed in each area, listing the assets in that location. A transfer listing should support the location listing to note any movement of the asset. These listing are to be checked periodically. Once the asset is permanently moved from an area, the location listing is to be updated.

Establishing a Board

"Nobody can go back and start a new beginning, but anyone can start today and make a new ending."

~ Maria Robinson

CIIR (2005) indicated that Member Organizations may specify in their governance documents the number of members to represent the governing body, either as trustees with voting rights or as non-voting members (observers). A member organization must have a clear provision regarding membership and should cover eligibility to become a member, which could be an individual or an organization, the fees to be paid (subscription), voting rights, and termination of membership. Members should be terminated only when there is a good and sufficient reason to terminate, the matter is explained to the individual concerned, and members get a hearing before final decisions are made. Members must exercise their membership rights only in the interest of the organization and not for personal gain.

The Church operates as a member organization, and so some of the practices governing a member organization may be adopted and applied to the establishment of a Board. One key thing to avoid is selecting people to lead based on the size of their offering, their business skill, or those who talk the most. The church needs people of integrity but also people who are saved and sanctified to manage the affairs of the church. Where the people selected are not fully prepared, they could seek further training or consult other church leaders who they associate with for guidance.

The Board is expected to carry out particular functions. Kerr (2005) also noted that there are five functions of an effective Board: value creation, monitoring, regulatory and legislative conformity, management issues, and ambassadorial. Thus, strengthening the independence and oversight provided by directors of publicly traded companies is the primary solution offered to avoid the occurrence of a future "Enron" (Macey, 2011).

Enron is an American corporation that collapsed. The collapse affected thousands of employees and shook Wall Street to its core. At Enron's peak, its shares were worth US$90.75; when it declared bankruptcy on December 2, 2001, they were trading at US$0.26. For several years Enron hid its losses, so the company would appear to be more profitable than it really was.

Many Boards of Directors failed in exercising their duty of care, failing to uncover behavior which even a minimum investigation would have shown to be damaging or illegal (Capaldi, 2005). Given the failure of Boards within the business arena, the church must ensure this does not happen to its operation by being proactive and decisive in establishing a credible and functional Board.

Swartley (2005) stated that all elders shared in the governance of New Testament churches. Unlike businesses, the church traditionally uses internal people for the board members. However, these board members of the church would have similar responsibilities as a business, in terms of their duty of care, controlling, directing, and monitoring.

Using an internal person may not be a bad thing, as they may be familiar with the operation, policy, doctrine, history, and culture of the church compared to an outsider. However, care should be taken to ensure those nominated and selected are competent and qualified to carry out the business of the church. Board members should add value to the governance structure of the church instead of stifling or hampering the effective operation of the church.

Having a mixed Board of in-house and external leaders could be ideal, as it could lead to greater governance as stated by Gillan (2006). However, because most churches are private in its operations, leaders may not be comfortable including external directors. The church therefore loses out on the benefits that could have been derived if an external director were included as a board member. The external director could bring more innovation, creativity, and experience to the table than the internal leaders possess. With a term limit, the external director can serve for a selected time and then a new director can be appointed, or the current external director could be reappointed based on his or her performance. With that said, there should be no fear in a church considering incorporating external directors and embracing a mixed board culture. The current leader could gain more insights and knowledge by working with other talent.

Here are some guidelines that may be relevant when establishing a Board or selecting directors for a Board:

Key Qualities of the Director

- Spiritually sound
- Understand the mission and vision of the church
- Knowledge of church governance and administration
- Commitment of time
- Provide feedback – critical, timely, substantial
- Attend board meetings and fully participate
- Realize that his/her first duty is to the church
- Be part of a 'champion team' rather than a 'team of champions'
- Support other directors

Core Value of the Director

- Unquestionable integrity
- Passing rigid 'fit-and-proper' standards
- Vigour and vitality – sufficient to do the job
- Skills
- Intelligence
- Free from a material connection or anything that could lead to tension and mistrust between the directors

Competencies of the Director

- Specific-experience and church knowledge
- Apply strategic thought-processes in critical thinking
- Ability to think objectively and to use objective criteria in problem-solving
- Problem-solving aptitude and commercial skills
- Monitoring and probing abilities
- Corporate governance mindset
- Social graces and networking skills
- Team skills and people-oriented
- Stakeholder orientation and focus
- Board value-added capabilities

- Value-added business skills
- Flexibility
- Educational training
- Spiritual alertness

Function of the Board

- Value creation – provide stern, fair, and uncompromising leadership. Having a futuristic view (Strategic foresight of mission, vision, values, strategy, opportunities). Provide useful feedback.
- Monitoring
- Regulatory and legislative conformity
- Management issues – members and local communities forecast, mitigate, and manage crises.
- Ambassadorial – represent the church at high-level negotiations, heads legal regulatory issues, and responsible for media-related issues.

SUMMARY OF GUIDELINES

1) Select people of integrity and competence who are qualified, saved, and sanctified to be on the church board. These people will have the duty of care, controlling, directing, and monitoring responsibility.

2) Ensure board members are adequately trained and seek help from other church leaders when needed.

3) Five functions of an effective board are value creation, monitoring, regulatory and legislative conformity, management issues, and ambassadorial.

4) The church does not have to fear implementing a mixed board culture of external and internal directors. External directors can bring more innovation, creativity, and experience. To deal with any fear, leaders can set term limits and reappoint directors based on performance.

5) In selecting board members, there are key qualities, core values, competencies, and functions that the candidate should meet.

Importance of Meeting

"Success is doing what you want, when you want, where you want, with whom you want, as much as you want."

~ Anthony Robbins

In relation to the frequency of Board meetings and members' meetings, all the churches in the study have Board meetings, periodically. Members' meetings for six of the churches are held at set intervals, while at the other four churches, these are held as the need arises. The need is mainly dependent on upcoming events, so members can be informed or be able to discuss plans. Another reason for meeting is an urgent or important issue to be addressed, which could be motivated by the leaders or the members. Overall, there was evidence of meetings being held, although the frequency of meetings varied among churches.

The churches appeared to be doing well in the area of convening Board meetings and members' meetings. However, it would be instructive to hear the views of the wider congregation. As such, further research could be undertaken in this area. This is necessary because there were some discrepancies noted in the documentation review about those meetings.

Here are some guidelines to help in planning and conducting meetings:

Planning Meetings

- It is important that leaders of the church meet and plan.
- You can plan the activities for the year, quarter, month, or week.
- Tasks can be assigned to people (delegation) or plans can be made together (collectively).
- You can decide on resource people to contact for assistance.

- Where assistance is needed, identify this early so that those who will be called on to help can make personal plans to take on the task.
- As individual leaders, plan your area of responsibility as well as identify things needed by the overall church.
- Bring your plans and thoughts to the leadership meetings for further discussion, approval, and implementation.

Importance of Leadership Meetings

- This helps the leaders to be on one accord.
- The burden of finding ideas and things to do is shared.
- The leaders get to work together better.
- Matters can be discussed which are not for the general membership.
- Allow for reviews so you can learn from mistakes.
- A meeting should have an agenda – this gives direction to the meeting and ensures you cover the areas intended. It also suggests careful planning.

Agenda

This will vary depending on the meetings, the time available, and the urgency of the matters to be discussed. The agenda could include the following:

- Call to order – The chairperson will call the meeting to order and state the reason for the meeting or what it will cover.
- Devotion – Notify someone beforehand to do this or it could be done by the chairperson. Prayer is key for all church meetings.
- Welcome – If not done at the call to order, you could now state the reason for the meeting or what it will cover. It could be done by the chairperson or someone who was previously notified. Affirm the attendance of the participants, especially new people or those who have not been at meetings for an extended time.
- Roll Call – The secretary will call the names; this is usually done in general meetings. However, at the leadership meeting, the secretary would note the attendees and absentees on the minutes.

- ➢ <u>Minutes of the Previous Meeting</u> – This will be read by the secretary for general meetings. For leadership meetings, the minutes are to be circulated prior to the date of the next meeting.
- ➢ <u>Matters Arising from the Minutes</u> – People can get clarification or updates on anything mentioned in the minutes or on projects in progress. People who were assigned tasks at the last meeting will give feedback or update on their tasks.
- ➢ <u>New Business</u> – Here new matters will be raised and reported.
- ➢ <u>Any Other Business (A.O.B.)</u> – Here the general membership can raise new matters that have not been raised in the meeting. It is ideal that these are shared with the chairperson beforehand for better control of the meeting.
- ➢ <u>Adjournment</u> – At this point, the closing is done. Generally, church meetings are closed with prayer, but a song could be done before the prayer.

Yearly/Quarterly Activities

- Yearly and quarterly activities are the things the department can reasonably manage for the period.
- Plan activities based on the number of people available, plan them with a specific focus in mind, based on what the department can afford, identify the right timing, identify the right audience.
- When these are planned long in advance, they give you enough time to get things in place before the actual date.
- Share the plans with the team, get them involved in developing the activities.

Here are some guidelines to help in planning for a major service:

- Establish a committee and hold meetings to assign people to work on the various areas.
- Determine the date of the event.
- Identify the venue – Assess the grounds, ease of transportation, fans, décor, affordability, hygiene, adequate seating, etc.

- Determine the number of people to cater for.
- Determine the theme and sub-themes – supported by relevant scripture references.
- Contact speakers verbally to get their availability and follow up with a written invitation. Telephone close to the date to confirm. Always have a backup plan. Provide relevant information in time for the presenter to prepare him/herself. These also apply to singers invited to minister at the event or for concerts.
- Determine a token/love offering/fee for the guest speaker or gospel artist – this depends on your relationship with the person and the person's policy.
- Ensure a PA System (microphone) is in place and musicians are arranged, whether in-house or invited – musicians must be spiritually sound and be aware of your standards.
- Determine the features and items for the event – work out a timetable of the days' activities. Always have a goal in mind.

➢ Determine the menu – Identify people to work in this area, items to be purchased, preparation of the meal, and clean up. Take note of people with special diets or allergies. A catered service is ideal, though costly. You could also invite concessionaires to the event to sell their products or food items.

➢ Hospitality/Logistics – Identify people to cater for the invited guests. The usher team can help in this area. Ensure seats are in place, the bathroom is intact, and all grounds are covered before and during the event.

➢ Prepare Letters of Invitation and have them mailed or delivered on time – at least two months before for new events and one month for annual events that occur on a fixed date. Special guests and speakers/presenters must be invited much earlier before the general invitations are sent.

➢ Prepare the program/song sheets – Use relevant songs in keeping with the theme. Determine whether these program/song sheets will be given free or at a cost. Identify key people for the events: moderator, individuals or groups to do items, selections, tributes or greetings, etc.

- Budget and Financial Control – Develop a budget for the event, inflows expected (contributions or fundraising efforts), and the outflows (expenses that will be incurred). Manage the payments of the bills closely. Fundraising could be done in advance of the event to help finance the project. For the General Convention, a fee could be determined, which members are encouraged to pay. This can be used to finance the Convention, which includes making a contribution to speakers and presenters, providing meals for guests, catering to members' accommodation, among other things.

- Where tickets are being used at an event, determine the price to sell tickets and print them in time to have them sold – look out for fraudulent tickets.

SUMMARY OF GUIDELINES

1) The importance of meeting must not be taken lightly. It is needed for planning, to gather information, to communicate ideas, to build relationships, to facilitate updates, and to allow for reviews of past activities in terms of progress made or areas of weakness.

2) Leaders or board members should be given tasks at meetings which they will report on in subsequent meetings. They can also provide updates or feedback for the team on other important matters.

3) An agenda gives direction to meetings and areas to cover, which suggests careful planning.

4) When planning activities, do so based on the resources available, what you can afford, the right timing, and the right target group.

5) Planning major services can be overwhelming if not done properly (see detailed guidelines given in this Chapter).

6) Planning the financial aspects of an event is important to ensure all expenses are covered. Inflows can be generated by doing fundraising activities, collecting a fee or contribution, or with the use of tickets at the gate (look out for fraudulent tickets).

Risk Management

"Risk must be taken, because the greatest hazard in life is to risk nothing."

~ Leo Buscaglia

When the study was done among the churches, risk management was not included. However, the importance of risk management came to light during the defense of the dissertation.

Enterprise Risk Management

The church can take a broad perspective on identifying the risks that could cause it to fail to meet its strategies and objectives. Brehm, Paul, et al. (2007) defined enterprise risk management as "the process of identifying critical risks, quantifying their impacts on the company's strategy and implementing integrated strategies to maximize firm value." The church as an enterprise can adopt and implement this approach as part of good administration.

Managing risks is a key element of an organization. Risk is defined as an uncertain event or condition that, if it occurs, has a positive or negative effect on one or more objectives of the organization. Risk tends to be greater where there is a lack of experience, lack of knowledge, and uncertainties because new avenues are being taken. Therefore, the risk can take various forms, such as liquidity, operational, financial, or institutional.

Liquidity Risk

Liquidity risk is where the church is unable to meet its payment obligations associated with its financial liabilities. Managing liquidity is to ensure, as far as possible, that the church will always have sufficient liquidity to meet its liabilities when due, under both normal and stressed conditions, without incurring unacceptable losses or risking damages to the church's reputation.

Operational Risk

Operational risk is the risk of direct or indirect loss arising from a wide variety of causes associated with the church's processes, personnel, technology, and infrastructure, and from external factors other than credit, market, and liquidity risks such as those arising from legal and regulatory requirements and generally accepted standards of corporate behavior. Operational risks arise from all of the church's operations. Therefore, leaders of the church should undertake the management of operational risks.

Financial Risk

This is any of the various types of risk associated with financing, including financial transactions that include company loans in risk of default. Financial risk covers: Credit Risk, Liquidity Risk, Market Risk, and Operation Risk.

Institutional Risk

Institutional risks are those risks that could prevent the organization from achieving its objectives, inherent in pursuing the mission, and must be appropriately managed as part of the overall strategic planning process. Institutional risk management is also known as enterprise risk management.

Often, there are known risks, those that are identified and analyzed, and it may be possible to plan for those risks. Unknown risks cannot be managed proactively, and a prudent response by the team can be to allocate a general contingency against such risks. Risk responses reflect an organization's perceived balance between risk-taking and risk-avoidance.

Risk Management

The goal of risk management is to increase the probability and impact of positive events and decrease the probability and impact of adverse events to any project.

Risk management is the systematic process of identifying, analyzing, and responding to risk. It involves managing the core processes and utilizing and applying techniques, which result in certain outputs. Managing risks benefits the organization by increasing visibility, providing a competitive advantage, and generating personal success.

Failing to manage risk may have two kinds of negative consequences, as follows:

1) Failing to meet technical objectives. This may lead to cost overruns, delays, cancellation, penalties, damages, personal and/or organizational liabilities, loss of credibility, and loss of market share.
2) Missing opportunities to exceed the objectives. This happens where there is a failure to take advantage of opportunities.

There are seven principles of risk management, which are as follows:

1) Cost Benefit Analysis – Here we look at the expenditure of the risk in relation to the impact it would have on the organization. Realized risk is the impact to the organization if the risk actually occurs, which may be a financial loss, delays in completion, and missed opportunities or inability to achieve a requirement or objective.
2) Organizational Context and Objectives – A church can be affected by political, social, legal, or societal factors. Therefore, risk management should add value, be an integral part of the organizational process, and explicitly address the uncertainty.

3) Grade Approach – This allows flexibility to choose risk management approaches, controls, and tools with varying levels of rigor to manage risk. It is a management tool used to determine where to assign appropriate resources, help define scope, evaluate risk elements, and get a consensus from the team responsible to implement and manage it.

4) Open Communication – The risk management should be transparent and inclusive, taking into account the human factors and ensuring that each one knows his/her roles at each stage of the process. Information must flow freely, the authenticity of the information must be ascertained, and a wide variety of communication modes must be used to ensure information is not restricted based on preference.

5) Integrated Risk Management – This is a culture that embeds risk management into day-to-day activities and ensures systems are in place to manage risk. In addition, an integrated approach ensures risk management is integrated throughout

the entire operation of the church. All the meetings held should include a risk component, and each leader should understand his intervention at each stage of the operational lifecycle.

6) Team Approach – This is a best practice, as all the leaders can participate. The leader of the team with ideas regarding the risk and its impact can meet to develop the risk responses. It would involve stakeholders at every step of the decision-making process and being aware of all the decisions.

7) Apply Continuous Processes and Improvement – Here, inputs are evaluated at each step of the risk management process. In doing so, one must identify, assess, respond, and review. The observations at each cycle should be reviewed to identify reasonable interventions and remove unnecessary ones. The risk management team must be empowered and capable of improving and enhancing the risk management strategies and tactics as well as maintaining adequate monitoring sources, which provide alerts regarding emerging risks.

Identifying the risk is the process of determining which risks may affect the organization and documenting their characteristics.

The process involved a documentation review to determine inconsistency or lack of clarity. Missing information and inconsistencies are indicators of a hidden risk. Information gathering is another technique used to develop lists of risks and risk characteristics. This can be done through brainstorming, the Delphi technique (gaining information from experts, anonymously about the likelihood of future events/risks occurring), interviewing, and root cause identification.

A SWOT Analysis can be done as part of the risk identification and analysis. A SWOT Analysis is a strategic planning technique that examines the strengths, weaknesses, opportunities, and threats to the organization. Strengths and weaknesses include that of the leaders, the church, and the projects being done. These are internal skills and resources, or areas that require improvements. Opportunities are external situations from which benefits can be derived when the organizational internal strengths are applied. Threats, on the other hand, are also external, but they are events with the potential to magnify the weaknesses.

Expert judgment can be applied to the risk management process. The expert can use their training and experience to identify risks throughout the church's operation. However, the experts' potential bias must always be assessed.

Having completed the process of identifying the risk process, a Risk Register can be done. A Risk Register is the documentation in which the results of risk analysis and risk response planning are recorded. It contains the outcomes of the other risk management processes as they are conducted, resulting in an increase in the level and type of information contained in the Risk Register over time.

Qualitative risk analysis can be done on all the risks. This is the process of prioritizing risks for further analysis or action by assessing and combining their probability of occurrence and impact. Here the risks are prioritized for the Planned Risk Responses process.

Plan Risk Responses is the process of developing options and actions to enhance opportunities and to reduce threats to project objectives. The techniques to be applied are as follows:

1. **Strategies for Negative Risks or Threats**
   a) Avoid the risk – Eliminate the root cause or change plan to eliminate the risk.
   b) Transfer the risk – Done by shifting the impact of the risk to another party (Get insurance coverage).
   c) Mitigate the risk – Here you minimize the probability and/or impact of an adverse risk.
   d) Accept the risk – This can be active (having a contingency reserve to deal with the effects should the risk materialize) or passive (nothing is done).

2. **Strategies for Positive Risks or Opportunities**
   a) Exploit – Selected where the organization wishes to ensure that the opportunity is realized.
   b) Share – This is allocating ownership to a third party who is best able to capture the opportunity for the benefit.
   c) Enhance – This modifies the size of an opportunity by increasing probability and/or positive impacts and by identifying and maximizing key drivers of these positive-impact risks.
   d) Accept – This is being willing to take advantage of it should the opportunity occur.

3. **Contingent Response Strategies**

This is used only if certain events occur. It is executed under specific predefined conditions. It is important to define and track all events triggering contingency.

4. **Expert Judgment**

This entails the application of specialized knowledge to the Plan Risk Response process. This includes other departments, consultants, professional associations, and subject-matter experts.

Managing risks is an ongoing process, as one must continuously monitor for new and changing risks. Control Risks is the process of implementing risk response plans, tracking identified risks, monitoring residual risks, identifying new risks, and evaluating risk process effectiveness throughout the organization. Risk control techniques, such as variance and trend analysis can be applied. These techniques require the use of performance data generated at different intervals.

It is obvious that a lot of information has been shared regarding risk management. This is to give leaders an idea on how broad risk management is and, therefore, further training may be needed.

A church involves the regular gathering of many people, relatively expensive equipment, important records/documentation, and a building that may be old. There are inherent risks in all these areas, so one of the best suggestions is to have adequate insurance in place to deal with all the possible events that may arise to negatively affect the church (transfer the risk).

SUMMARY OF GUIDELINES

1) Attention must be given to risk management, as it can positively or negatively impact the organization.

2) As an enterprise, the church should identify critical risks, quantify their impact on the church's strategy, and implement integrated strategies to maximize the church's value. The leaders should mitigate negative risks but capitalize on positive risks.

3) There are various kinds of risks, and these risks are greater where there is a lack of experience, knowledge, or uncertainties, especially in new avenues. There are liquidity, operational, financial, or institutional risks.

4) Risk management involves identifying, analyzing, and responding to risks. These comprise of seven principles (see details provided in this Chapter).

5) In identifying risks, look for those risks that may affect the organization and document their characteristics. A SWOT analysis can help in identifying and analyzing risks. This strategic planning technique examines the strengths, weaknesses, opportunities, and threats of the organization.

6) Use a Risk Register to document the risk analysis and risk response results. The risk response will vary based on the nature and type of risks; further details are presented in this Chapter.

7) Managing risks is an ongoing process that involves looking for new and changing risks. Having adequate insurance in place is an ideal way to handle certain risks, as it transfers the problem from the church to the insurance company.

CHAPTER 15

DEALING WITH DESTRUCTIVE CONFLICTS

"Life is not about waiting for the storms to pass. It's about learning how to dance in the rain."

~ Vivian Greene

The pastors purported several ways corporate governance can prevent destructive conflicts. The responses noted that corporate governance fosters a written documentation of policies and procedures and results in a clearer understanding of roles and responsibilities. Members are provided a channel to discuss issues, noting that members' adherence to corporate governance is crucial. The responses also indicated that corporate governance reduces segregation and allows younger people to succeed as leaders and helps to better manage the change. Good communication and unity among the church body can be achieved with corporate governance, which eliminates confusion, and people can appreciate decisions easier.

Pinson (2010) stated that the Baptist congregational church purports a governance structure that often led to destructive conflicts. Throughout the interviews, it was revealed that some of the churches which participated in the study experienced some destructive conflicts, such as divisions within the church and challenges when there is a change of leadership. Destructive conflicts are issues that must constantly be managed. Incidentally, the pastors made some direct suggestions on how corporate governance prevents this. More importantly, they emphasized that corporate governance aids in this process, leads to a better understanding, eliminates confusion, and provides a platform on which disagreements and grievances can be dealt with. These points confirm the need for small churches to ensure that good corporate governance is implemented. The pastors should therefore embrace these points and promote them within their denominations as a means of advocating greater unity. Bickers (2005) posited that conflicts cannot be avoided in the church and that those unresolved will resurface and result in stagnation.

Corporate governance can also minimize divisiveness and ensure that there are greater controls and more professionalism. Many pastors see corporate governance as a tool to prevent destructive conflicts, while one pastor indicated "it [corporate governance] provides a platform on which disagreements and grievances can be dealt with."

Various themes emerged from the responses provided by the participants. Two pastors described the need for written documentation to be in place for all to follow. Most of the respondents indicated that effective communication can prevent destructive conflicts. A few of the respondents indicated that unification and inclusiveness are good ways to prevent destructive conflicts. One pastor noted that greater professionalism prevented destructive conflicts, while two pastors noted a better system and structure to prevent destructive conflicts.

Within the church, and especially among the leaders, there should be teamwork, but often challenges arise. Churches with a solid organizational structure and a firm teaching of the Bible are not exempt from conflict. Conflict is a people problem, which can be distinguished as individual and group interests, personality problems, and problem people. Conflict, from a project management perspective, is defined as a pattern of opposition between people (or group of people) that positively or negatively affects something important. Conflict is commonly caused by project priorities; goals, and objectives; administrative procedures; personality conflicts; lack of respect for each other; technical opinions and performance; staffing resources; cost; and schedules.

Conflict may present opportunities for improvement and can be categorized as cognitive and affective. Cognitive conflicts aim at issues, ideas, principles, or processes, and they are thus constructive and functional, while affective conflicts, on the other hand, aim at people, emotions, or values, and they are thus destructive and dysfunctional.

Functional conflict indicates something is wrong, stimulates change, encourages creativity, diffuses more serious conflict, improves performance, leads to the change and personal growth of members, results in a solution to a problem, increases the involvement of everyone affected by the conflict, and builds cohesiveness among the team.

Dysfunctional conflict causes stress, lowers productivity, distorts behavior, causes loss of status or position, prevents a decision from being reached—meaning the problem still exists, diverts energy away from more value-added activities, destroys the morale of the team members, and polarizes or divides the team.

As a church, different stakeholders may have different priorities; therefore, the conflict can involve members of the church, department or ministries within the church, projects conflicting with each other, the church and the community it serves, the leader and members of the church, and the church needs versus the members personal needs.

In dealing with conflict, proactive conflict management strategies can be applied. This is a preventative mechanism and includes the following:

- Implement team ground rules.
- Develop a conflict resolution plan and agreement.
- Solid leadership, which involves communication and role definition.
- Training in conflict management.

There is also a reactive-conflict management strategy which is used when a conflict has occurred. This is to withdraw, avoid, make a decision without the participation of those involved (split justice), and smoothing/accommodating.

Understanding various conflict resolution techniques is important for all leaders of the church. There are six general techniques for resolving team conflict, as listed below:

1. <u>Withdrawal/Avoiding</u> – This is temporary and will not resolve the issue. It is postponing an issue for later or withdrawing from the situation altogether. With this approach, the problem and conflict will continue to reoccur repeatedly. This approach is used when you know you cannot win, stakes are low, you are not prepared, to gain time, to maintain neutrality or reputation, or to win by delaying.

2. <u>Smoothing/Accommodating</u> – This is temporary and will not resolve the issue, but it is generally used when tension is high. It is also referred to as the obliging style. Here the areas of agreement are emphasized, and the areas of disagreement are downplayed. A person may sacrifice his or her own

concerns or goals to satisfy the concerns or goals of the other party. It is used when the goal to be reached is overarching, liability is limited, any solution is adequate, to be harmonious or to create goodwill, where you would lose anyway if another method should be utilised, or when you want to gain time.

3. <u>Compromising/Reconciling</u> – This provides resolution. It is a give-and-take style in which parties bargain to reach a mutually acceptable solution. Both parties give up something to reach the decision, but also leave with some degree of satisfaction (win-win). It is used when both parties need to win, you are in a deadlock, time is not sufficient, to maintain the relationship among the involved parties, you get nothing without compromising, and stakes are moderate.

The advantages include faster resolution; may be more practical when time is a factor; can provide a temporary solution while still looking for a win-win solution; and lowers the levels of tension and stress resulting from the conflict. However, caveats to bear in mind are that it may result in a situation where both parties are not satisfied with the outcome (a lose-lose situation); does not contribute to building trust in the long run; and may require close monitoring and control to ensure the agreements are met.

4. <u>Force/Direct</u> – This provides resolution and is also known as a competing, controlling, or dominating style. It occurs when one party goes all out to win its position while ignoring the needs and concerns of the other party. As the intensity of a conflict increases, the tendency for a forced conflict is more likely. This may result in a win-lose situation where one party wins at the expense of the other party. It is used when no alternative situation is present, stakes are high, important principles are at stake, the relationship between parties is not important, or a quick decision must be made. Caveats to bear in mind are that it may negatively affect your relationship with the opponent, cause the opponent to react in the same way, and may require a lot of energy and be exhausting to some individuals.

5. <u>Collaborating</u> – With this approach, a consensus is required. It involves an attempt to work the other person to find a win-win solution to the problem at hand – the one that most satisfies the concerns of both parties. It includes identifying the underlying concerns of the opponents and finding an alternative which meets each party's concerns. Collaboration and problem-solving are closely linked and should be used when the consensus and commitment of the other parties is important, in a collaborative environment, it is required to address the interests of multiple stakeholders, a high level of trust is present, a long-term relationship is important, you need to work through hard feelings, animosity, etc., and you don't want full responsibility.

Caveats to bear in mind are that it requires a commitment from all parties to look for a mutually acceptable solution; may require more effort and more time than other methods; may not be practical when timing is crucial and a quick solution or fast response is required; and once one or more parties lose their trust in an opponent, the relationship falls back to other methods of conflict resolution; therefore, a collaborative relationship is needed from all parties.

6. <u>Problem-solving</u> – This provides the best resolution. It involves the parties meeting face-to-face and collaborating to reach an agreement that satisfies the concerns of both parties. This style involves open and direct communication, which should lead to solving the problem. It is used when both parties need to win, you want to decrease cost, you want to create a common power base, skills are complementary, time is sufficient, trust is present, and learning is the ultimate goal.

Caveats to bear in mind are that it requires a commitment from all parties to look for a mutually acceptable solution, more effort and more time than some other methods, a win-win solution may not be evident, and may not be practical when timing is crucial, and a quick solution or fast response is required.

When applying a conflict resolution technique, the following steps can be taken:

1. Ease the tension – This involves listening without judgment; remaining calm, absorbing hostility, not reacting; listening, not offering solutions; expressing understanding and concern; and focusing on the problem, not the person.
2. Research the problem – Ask questions to identify conflict participants, problem, preferred state, and common ground.
3. Explore and evaluate options – Work together to find the resolution that works best for both parties by brainstorming ways to resolve the conflict, evaluating the options of the brainstorming exercise, and selecting the best options.
4. Develop an implementation plan – complete the three parts of an implementation plan, which are: describe each step, identify the responsible person, and select a due date.
5. Follow up and adjust as needed – Identify evaluation criteria by asking, "How will we know if the solution is working?" Set a date for the follow-up, evaluate the process, and adjust the plan only if necessary.

Summary of Guidelines

1) Destructive conflicts are issues that must constantly be managed because, when avoided or left unresolved, they can resurface at another time.

2) Good corporate governance practices within the organization will help minimize conflict if all parties follow them.

3) Conflict comes in the form of individual/group interests, personality problems, or problem people.

4) Within the church, each stakeholder may have different priorities, hence the possibility of a conflict arising.

5) A proactive conflict management mechanism should be in place, which includes team ground rules, a conflict resolution plan and agreement, solid leadership with communication and role definition, and training in conflict management.

6) A reactive conflict management strategy comprises withdrawing, avoiding, making decisions without those involved, and smoothing/accommodating.

7) There are six general techniques for resolving team conflicts: withdrawal/avoiding, smoothing/accommodating, compromising/reconciling, force/direct, collaborating, and problem-solving.

8) When applying the conflict resolution technique, the steps to follow are: ease the tension, research the problem, explore and evaluate options, develop an implementation plan, and follow up and adjust the plan as needed.

Network Among Churches

"Seek opportunity, not security. A boat in a harbour is safe, but in time its bottom will rot out."

~ H. Jackson Brown, Jr.

Mixed views were present among the respondents in terms of the need for a unified and structured governance model for Jamaica. Based on the findings presented, the researcher is of the view that the churches could collaborate to deal with those important issues to ensure that good corporate governance is being practiced among all the respective churches. Toon et al. (2004) show the division of churches regarding church polity (church government); therefore, introducing a unified and structured governance model among small churches can be challenging.

The participants shared various views on the issue of having a unified/structured governance model for Jamaica. Those who responded positively described that a unified/structured governance model will promote harmony and cooperation; leaders can collectively work and help each other; it will strengthen the effectiveness of the churches; help to curtail churches operating loosely; and relinquish confusion and division among the body of Christ. Only one pastor clearly responded negatively toward the unified/structured governance model; he believed the model would stifle growth. Pastors, who were indifferent to the issue of the unified/structured governance, believe each church has a different mandate, and the governance model would evolve from those mandates. One pastor indicated the need for all to learn to appreciate differences. Those who are indifferent also believe that implementing a unified/structured governance model would be challenging.

In light of this, having a unified/structured governance model for Jamaica is almost impossible at the moment. It may take years before this can be achieved. This may only happen if the government decides to implement a regulatory arm for the church. Notwithstanding, I strongly recommend that a denomination or group of churches should ensure that a common governance structure is in place. This will be fuelled by its own policies, procedures, and doctrines. However, these should be developed from an informed position and in keeping with best practices.

Generally, churches in Jamaica associate or affiliate with other churches, such as those in the community in which it serves or other similar ministries. Therefore, regarding governance matters, church leaders could network among themselves for knowledge and insight on how to deal with particular issues at hand. It is unwise for a church to be struggling when help can be sought externally. In fact, the church belongs to God, and He must be sought for help and direction at all times.

SUMMARY OF GUIDELINES

1) Churches within a body or those that associate and/or affiliate with each other, can meet and collaborate on important issues for better governance /administration of the church. They can network among themselves for knowledge and insight.

2) From the study, there are mixed views regarding a unified or structured governance model for Jamaican churches. It is clear that this would be challenging to develop and implement at this time.

3) Church leaders should always be mindful of any government regulatory changes that are relevant to the church and adhere to them.

4) Within a denomination or group of churches, it is ideal to have a common governance structure, which is fuelled by its own policies, procedures, and doctrines.

5) Developing governance practices must be done from an informed position and in keeping with best practices at all times.

References

1. ACCA. (2002). Strategic business planning and development. Study text paper 3.5. London, UK: BPP.
2. AICD (2013). Good governance principles and guidance for NFP organizations. Retrieved from: http://www.companydirectors.com.au/director-resource-centre/not-for-profit/good-governance-principles-and-guidance-for-nfp-organizations
3. Akin, D., Brand, C., & Norman, R. (2004). Perspectives on church government. Nashville, Tennessee: Broadman & Holman.
4. Aguilera, R., Filatotchev, I., Gospel, H., & Jackson, G. (2008). An organizational approach to comparative corporate governance: Costs, contingencies, and complementarities. Organization Science, 19(3), 475-492.

5. Anheier, H. K. (2005). Nonprofit organizations: Theory, management, policy. Routledge, London; New York.
6. Anthony, J., & Middlebrook, D. (2014). The 7 building blocks of the 21st-century church. Grapevine, Texas: The Church Law Group. Retrieved from: http://www.churchlawgroup.com/governance.html
7. Babbie, E. R. (2004). The practice of social research. Belmont, CA: Wadsworth.
8. Bakker, J. (2011). Fall to grace: A revolution of God, self, and society. Retrieve from http://www.today.com/id/41019741/ns/today-today_books/t/fall-grace-life-son-jim-tammy-faye-bakker/#.VgqjZp1j_mI
9. Brehm, Paul, et al. (2007). "Enterprise Risk Analysis for property & Liability Insurance Companies" – A Practical Guide to Standard Models and Emerging Solutions.
10. Beech, H. (2011). The Dalai Lama promises to clarify his succession—when he's around 90. Retrieved from: http://world.time.com/2011/09/26/the-dalai-lama-promises-to-clarify-his succession%E2%80%94when-hes-around-90

11. Bickers, D. (2005). The healthy small church: Diagnosis and treatment for the big issues. Kansas City, MN: Beacon Hill Press.
12. Brealey, R., Myers, S., & Marcus, A. (2001). Fundamentals of corporate finance (3rd ed.). New York, NY: McGraw-Hill.
13. Bryan, A., & Bell, E. (2007). Business research methods (2nd ed..). New York, NY: Oxford University Press.
14. Business Dictionary 2017. Definition of Accountability. Web Finance Inc. Retrieved from: http://www.businessdictionary.com/definition/accountability.html
15. Byassee, J. (2010). The gifts of the small church (ministry in the small membership church). Nashville, TN: Abingdon Press.
16. Cadbury, A. (1992). The final report of the committee on the financial aspects of corporate governance-the code of best practice. London, UK: Gee and Co. Ltd.
17. Capaldi, N. (2005). Business and religion: A clash of civilizations? (Conflicts and trends in business ethics). Salem, MA: M & M Scrivener Press.

18. Carver, J. (2006). Boards that make a difference: A new design for leadership in non-profit and public organizations (3rd ed.). Hoboken, NJ: Jossey-Bass.
19. Channon, D. (1999). Encyclopedic dictionary of strategic management. Oxford, UK: Blackwell.
20. Charan, R., Drotter, S., & Noel, J. (2001). The leadership pipeline. San Francisco, CA: Jossey-Bass.
21. Charmaz, K. (2006). Constructing Grounded Theory: A practical guide through qualitative analysis. Thousand Oaks, CA: SAGE.
22. Chisholm, C. (2012). Religion and the 2011 census. Retrieved from http://jamaica-gleaner.com/gleaner/20121104/focus/focus4.html
23. Chronmey, R. (1995). Children's ministry guide for smaller churches. Loveland, CO: Group Publishing, Inc.
24. CIIR. (2005). Capacity building for NGOs: A guidance manual for good practice. Catholic Institute for International Relations, London, UK. Retrieved from: http://www.capacity.org/capacity/export/sites/capacity/documents/topic-readings/Capacity_Building_for_Local_NGOs__A_Guidance_Manual_for_Good_Practicex1x.pdf

25. CIMA. (2004.) Organization management and information systems. Study text paper P.4. Wokingham, Berkshire: FTC Foulks Lunch.
26. Clarke, T. (2004). Theories of corporate governance: The philosophical foundation of corporate governance. Retrieved from http://www.centrostudilogos.com/news_ita/upload/uploads/theoriesOfCorporateGovernancePreface.pdf
27. Cornforth, C. (2012). Nonprofit governance research: Limitations of the focus on boards and suggestions for new directions, Nonprofit and Voluntary Sector Quarterly, 41(6), pp. 1116–1135.
28. Crandall, R. (1995). Turnaround strategies for the small church. Nashville, Tennessee: Abingdon Press.
29. Creswell, J. (2012). Educational Research: Planning, Conducting, and Evaluating Quantitative and Qualitative Research (4th ed.). Boston, MA: Pearson.
30. Creswell, J. (2003). Research design: Qualitative, quantitative and mixed methods approaches (2nd ed.). Thousand Oaks, CA: Sage.

31. Daman, G. (2008). Shepherding the small church: A leadership guide for the majority of today's churches (2nd ed.). Grand Rapids, MI: Kregel Publications.

32. Deutsch, Y. (2005). The impact of Board composition on firms critical decisions: A meta-analytic review. Journal of Management, 31(3), 424-444.

33. Drucker, P. (2013). The nonprofit Drucker: performance and results: consensus and dissent, conflict, and feuding. Retrieved from: http://ccdl.libraries.claremont.edu/cdm/ref/collection/dac/id/5063

34. Drucker, P. (1990). Lessons for Successful Nonprofit Governance. Retrieve from: http://bjpa.org/Publications/downloadPublication.cfm?PublicationID=4262

35. Dudley, C. (1978). Making the small church effective. Nashville, TN: Abingdon Press.

36. Dudley, C. (2003). Effective small churches in the 21st century. Nashville, TN: Abingdon Press.

37. Elson, R., O'Callaghan, S., & Walker, J. (2006). Corporate governance in religious organizations: A study of current practices in the local church.

38. Presented at the Allied Academics International Conference, New Orleans. Retrieved from http://www.sbaer.uca.edu/research/allied/2006-neworleans/governmental_and_nfpi/1.pdf
39. Esterberg, K. G. (2002). Qualitative methods in social research. Boston, MA: McGraw-Hill.
40. Finegold, D., Benson, G., & Hecht, D. (2007). Corporate Boards and company performance: Review of research in light of recent reforms. The Authors Journal Compilation 15(5), Blackwell Publishing Ltd.
41 Flick, U. (2002). An introduction to qualitative research (2nd ed.). London, UK: Sage.
42. Galer, R. (2002). Prudent Pension Rule Standard for the Investment of Pension Fund Assets, Financial Market Trends No. 83. OECD, Paris.
43. Gallagher, T., & Andrew, J. (2003). Financial management and mastering finance (3rd ed.). Upper Saddle River, NJ: Prentice Hall.
44. Gillan, S. (2006). Recent developments in corporate governance: An overview. Journal of Corporate Finance, 12. Governancehub & Co-operatives. (2007). Governance and organizational structures. Retrieve from: http://docplayer.net/11455655-Governance-and-organizational-structures.html

45. Gregg, S. (2001). Stakeholder theory: What it means for corporate governance. Retrieved from: http://www.cis.org.au/images/stories/policy-magazine/2001-winter/2001-17-2-samuel-gregg.pdf
46. Hambrick, D., Werder, A., & Zajac, E. (2008). New directors in corporate governance Research. Corporate Governance 19(3), May-Jun, pp. 381-385. Retrieved from http://orgsci.journal.informs.org/content/19/3/381.full.pdf+html
47. Harrington, H., & Bertin, M. (2009). Corporate governance for small to mid-sized organizations. Chico, CA: Paton Professional.
48. Hayle, P. (2010). SME governance and succession planning (workshop manual). Kingston, Jamaica: Institute of Chartered Accountants of Jamaica.
49. Hitt, M., Black, S., & Porter, L. (2005). Management (1st ed.). Upper Saddle River, NJ: Pearson/Prentice Hall. HLWIKI International. (2014). Grounded theory. Retrieved from http://hlwiki.slais.ubc.ca/index.php/Grounded_theory
50. Huang, C., and Ho, Y. (2010). Historical research on corporate governance: A bibliometric analysis. African Journal of Business Management, 5(2), 276-284.

51. Huczynski, A., & Buchanan, D. (2007). Organizational behavior (6th ed.). Harlow, UK: Prentice Hall.

52. Jamali, D., Safieddine, A., and Rabbath, M. (2008). Corporate governance and corporate social responsibility synergies and interrelationships. Corporate Governance: An International Review, 16(5), 443-459. Blackwell Publishing, Ltd.

53. Johnson, R. (2004). Corporate governance what model is best suited for Jamaica? Retrieved from http://jamaica-gleaner.com/gleaner/20040620/business/business3.html

54. Juckett, A. (2010). ESOP Corporate Governance. Retrieved from: http://www.esoppartners.com/blog/bid/88848/ESOP-Corporate-Governance

55. Kaplan, R. (2010). Conceptual foundations of the balanced scorecard. Retrieved from: http://www.hbs.edu/faculty/Publication%20Files/10-074.pdf

56. Killen, J. (2005). Pastoral care in the small membership church. Nashville, TN: Abingdon Press.

57. Kerr, V. (2005). Effective corporate governance: An emerging market (Caribbean) perspective on governing corporations in a disparate world. Kingston, Jamaica: Centre for Corporate Governance & Competitive Strategy (GovStrat).

58. Kreider, L. (2008). House to house: Growing healthy small groups and house churches in the 21stcentury. Shippensburg, Pennsylvania: Destiny Image.

59. Leedy, P., & Ormrod, J. (2010) Practical research: Planning and design, (9th ed.). New York, NY: Merril.

60. Leedy, P., & Ormrod, J. (2001). Practical research: Planning and design (7th ed.). Upper Saddle River, NJ: Prentice-Hall.

61. Lincoln, Y., & Guba, E. (1985). Naturalistic Inquiry. Newbury Park, California: Sage.

62. Long, K. (2008). An Introduction to Corporate Governance for Private ESOP Companies. Chang, Ruthenberg & Long PC. Retrieved from: http://www.seethebenefits.com/showarticle.aspx?Show=677

63. Macey, J. (2011). Corporate governance: Promises kept, promises broken. Woodstock, Oxfordshire: Princeton University Press.

64. Mapatuna, P. (2010). Religion and governance in Sri Lanka. Retrieved from http://religurd.wordpress.com/articles/religion-and-governance-in-sri-lanka

65. McCahery, J., & Vermeulen, E. (2010). Corporate governance of non-listed companies. Oxford, UK: Oxford University Press.

66. McKenna, E., & Beech, N. (2002). Human research management: A concise analysis. Essex, UK: Pearson Education, Limited.

67. Mclachlan, P. (2005). Electing a Pope. Retrieved from: http://permalink.gmane.org/gmane.culture.region.india.goa/27964

68. McMurray, A., Islam, M., Sarros, J., & Pirola-Merlo, A. (2012). The impact of leadership on workgroup climate and performance in a nonprofit organization. Leadership & Organization Development Journal, 33(6).

69. Nieuwhof, C. (2015). 5 signs bad governance is stifling your church's growth and mission. Retrieved from: http://careynieuwhof.com/2015/05/5-signs-bad-governance-is-stifling-your-churches-growth-and-mission

70. Oakley, F., & Russett, B. (2004). Governance, accountability, and the future of the Catholic Church. London, UK: Continuum International Publishing Group Ltd.

71. O'Brien, B. (2010). Strategically small church, the: intimate, nimble, authentic, and effective. Minneapolis, Missouri: Bethany House.

72. Osborne, L. (2008). Sticky church (leadership network innovation series). Grand Rapids, MI: Zondervan.

73. Patterson, R. (1992). Effectively leading: A guide for all church leaders. Wheaton, IL: Evangelical Training Association.
74. Pinson, W. M. (2010). Baptist Congregational Church Governance: A Challenge. Retrieved from: http://www.baptistdistinctives.org/textonly12.html
75. PWC (2012). Family firm: A resilient model for the 21st century. Retrieved from: http://www.pwc.com/gx/en/pwc-family-business-survey/assets/pwc-family-business-survey-2012.pdf
76. PMGI (2016). Lecture notes for Mastery in applying project management. Kingston, Jamaica: Project Management Global Institute.
77. Rabstejnek, C. (2010). Governance on nonprofit boards: Why is it so hard to accomplish? Retrieved from: http://www.houd.info/governance.pdf
78. Rosenthal, L. (2012). Nonprofit Corporate Governance: The Board's Role. Retrieved from: http://corpgov.law.harvard.edu/2012/04/15/nonprofit-corporate-governance-the-boards-role
79. Salkind, N. J. (2006). Exploring research (6th ed.). Englewood Cliffs, NJ: Prentice Hall.
80. Schmelczer, M. (2009). Lecture notes on performance management. Swiss Management Center University. Zurich, Switzerland

81. Scott-Williams, T. (2011). Time for church. Retrieved from: http://www.jamaicaobserver.com/columns/Time-for-church_8322467
82. Searcy, N., & Thomas, K. (2006). Launch: Starting a new church from scratch. Ventura, California: Regal Books.
83. Serwinski (2014). Importance of corporate governance in ESOP companies. Retrieved from: http://www.financierworldwide.com/importance-of-corporate-governance-in-esop-companies/#.VhnhQ8tdHmI
84. Siebart, P. & Reichard, C. (2004). Corporate Governance of Nonprofit Organization, In Zimmer, A., Priller, E. and Freise, M. (Eds.), Future of civil society: Making Central European nonprofit organizations work, (1st ed.). VS Verlag für Sozialwissenschaften, Wiesbaden, pp. 271–296.
85. Simpson, S. (2008). Non-governmental organizations (NGOs) Boards and corporate governance: The Ghanaian experience. Corporate Ownership & Control, 6(2). Winter, pp. 89-98. Retrieved from: http://www.lib.academy.sumy.ua/library/C_O_C/Volume%206,%20issue%202,%20Winter%202008.pdf

86. STATIN. (2011). Population and Housing Census. Kingston, Jamaica: Statistical Institute of Jamaica Stetzer, E. & Dodson, M. (2007). Comeback Churches: How 300 churches turned around and yours can too. Nashville, TN: B & H Publishing Group.

87. Stevens, W. (1967). Doctrines of the Christian religion. Grand Rapids, MI: Eerdmans Publishing Co.

88. Swartley, R. (2005). Eldership in action: Through biblical governance of the church. Dubuque, IA: ECS Ministries

89. The Companies Act. (2004). AN ACT to Repeal and replace the Companies Act As passed by the Honourable House of Representatives. (Jamaica). Kingston, Jamaica: Jamaica Printing Services (1992) Ltd. (Government Printers). Retrieved from http://www.miic.gov.jm/Companies_Act_2004_v1.pdf

90. Thomlinson, N. (2006). Church governance: On bringing "politics" (back) in. The Hinge: A Journal of Christian Thought for the Moravian Church, 13(2). Spring, pp. 2-18 and 28. Retrieved from http://www.moravianseminary.edu/center/Hinge/13.2/13.2HINGE.pdf

91. Tichio, J. (2012). Greatest inspirational quotes: 365 days to more Happiness, Success, and Motivation. Lexington, Kentucky
92. Toon, P., Taylor, R., Patterson, P. & Waldron, S. (2004). Who runs the church? Grand Rapids, MI: Zondervan
93. Tyson, J. (2007). Administration in the small membership church (ministry in the small membership church). Nashville, TN: Abingdon Press.
94. Urlacher, P. (2008). New issues in corporate governance. New York, NY: Nova Science Publishers.
95. USA Churches. (2014). Church size. Retrieved from http://www.usachurches.org/church-sizes.htm
96. Waltz, M. (2005). First impressions: Creating wow experiences in your church. Loveland, CO: Nav Press Publishing Group.
97. Weil, Gotshal, and Manges, LLP (2012). The guide to not-for-profit governance Sponsored by the Not-for-Profit Practice Group and the Pro Bono Committee of Weil, Gotshal & Manges LLP. Retrieved from: http://www.pbpatl.org/wp-content/uploads/2012/10/NFPGuide_2012.pdf

98. Welsh, R. (2011). Church Administration: Creating efficiency for effective ministry (2nd ed.). Nashville, TN: B& H Publishing

99. Westhead, P., & Howorth, C. (2006). Ownership and management issues associated with family firm performance and company objectives. Family Business Review, 19(4), 301–316.

100. Williams, C. (2007). Research methods. Journal of Business and Economic Research. 5(3).

101. Yin, R. (1989). Case study research: Design and method. Newbury Park, CA: Sage.

www.ingramcontent.com/pod-product-compliance
Lightning Source LLC
Chambersburg PA
CBHW051101230426
43667CB00013B/2399